I0155942

Sir John Fortescue's
A Triumph of Banners

Sir John Fortescue's
A Triumph of Banners
The British Army and the War in Canada and the
United States of America 1812-14

J. W. Fortescue

LEONAUR

Sir John Fortescue's A Triumph of Banners
The British Army and the War in Canada and the United States of America 1812-14
by J. W. Fortescue

FIRST EDITION

Text taken from *A History of the British Army*

Leonaur is an imprint of Oakpast Ltd

Copyright in this form © 2016 Oakpast Ltd

ISBN: 978-1-78282-491-6 (hardcover)
ISBN: 978-1-78282-492-3 (softcover)

http://www.leonaur.com

Publisher's Notes

The views expressed in this book are not necessarily
those of the publisher.

Contents

CHAPTER 1

1812

On July 17th, 1812, the very day when Wellington invested the forts of Salamanca in Spain, the President and Congress of the United States passed an Act declaring war against Great Britain. The news did not come as a surprise to the authorities in Canada; for the arrogant speeches of American orators, had left little doubt as to the general drift of American policy; and as early as in January 1812 the governor had perceived the necessity for making preparations against an attack in the ensuing summer. But to understand the nature of these preparations it is necessary first to sketch very briefly the actual condition of the Colony and the nature of the frontier which separated it from its powerful neighbour.

Canada at this period was divided into two provinces: Lower Canada, which extended from the mouth of the St. Lawrence to the Ottawa River, with the seat of Government at Montreal; and Upper Canada, which name covered the whole of the country to north and westward of the Ottawa, with the seat of Government at York, the modern Toronto. The Lower province with a population of two hundred and fifty to three hundred thousand was practically French, and at this period by no means well affected. The people were not unnaturally fascinated by the supremacy to which France had attained under the leadership of Napoleon; they conceived the great emperor to be irresistible, and, deeming that it could be only a matter of time before he became master of Canada, they thought to curry favour with him by making themselves obnoxious to the British.

They possessed what are called free institutions and had no grievance whatever; but the ties of blood and of race drew them strongly to Napoleon's side; and, if the emperor could have landed four or five thousand men with plenty of muskets, he would have mastered

Lower Canada with little trouble, (Tupper's *Life of Brock*). It was, however, by no means so certain that the French colonists would view with equanimity an invasion of Americans. There was of course always the danger lest, if armed to resist such invasion, they might use their weapons first to shake off British rule, without thought of ulterior consequences; but it was more probable that a good number at any rate would come out readily to defend their homes against the troops of so insolent and boastful a body as the American Congress.

The people of Upper Canada were very widely different. They did not number eighty thousand; but about half of them were Loyalists who had been driven from their homes by the victorious party in the United States at the close of the War of Independence. They had been the cream of the population of the American Colonies, and had brought to their new homes, besides the qualities which had raised them to eminence in their former country, a very bitter feeling towards their aforetime countrymen. They did not consider that they had been beaten in the struggle: they felt with perfect justice that, without the help of France, the disloyal and revolutionary party would not have prevailed in 1781; and now that that same party had again allied itself with France—the tyrannous France of Napoleon—to harry them once more, they asked for nothing better than the opportunity of meeting their ancient enemies in fair fight.

The regular troops in the Canadas at this time consisted of the Eighth, Forty-First, Forty-Ninth and Hundredth Regiments of the British line, and the Tenth Royal Veteran battalion. There were also three battalions of Provincial Fencibles, the Newfoundland and the Canadian, both of them dating from 1803, and the Glengarry, which last had been raised in December 1811 from among the Highland settlers, and, being composed mainly of Roman Catholics, was on that account the more acceptable to the French colonists.

The four regular regiments were not far from four thousand strong, and in fair order; but from the necessity of splitting many of them up into small detachments to cover the posts on the frontier, it was difficult to keep the soldiers for long in good discipline. A battalion in Upper Canada was generally divided among eight different stations several hundred miles asunder, and remained thus scattered as a rule for three years until relieved. American agents, many of them the lowest of the low, swarmed around these posts, contrasting the rations and pay of the American Army with the humble allowances meted out to the British.

In 1803 the tendency to relaxed discipline, and the effort of a well-meaning but narrow-minded officer to check it by extreme severity, had resulted in a mutinous plot in the Forty-ninth, for which seven men had suffered death. Colonel Brock, who commanded that regiment, had thereupon recommended the formation of a Veteran battalion for duty in the outlying posts, to be composed of selected men of good character, who should be tempted to attach themselves to the country by a grant of two hundred acres of land apiece. The Tenth Royal Veterans, nearly seven hundred strong, had been sent out in 1807 with the idea of fulfilling these conditions. The Forty-Ninth, when its companies were brought together, soon recovered itself; the Eighth was already in excellent order; the Forty-First was a stout battalion of old soldiers, but unfortunate in its colonel; and the Hundredth was made up of fine young Protestant Irishmen, not ill-disciplined but a little wild. Altogether the Regulars, Veterans and Fencibles composed a by no means contemptible force of from six to seven thousand men.

The enormous length of the frontier, however, made such small numbers almost ridiculous, while its extraordinary nature practically compelled dispersion of force. The five inland seas, called by courtesy lakes, which formed the northern boundary between the United States and Canada, of necessity turned any war between the two countries into a maritime struggle, with the additional complication that, though these waters could carry the largest ships, the rapids of the St. Lawrence, which river formed to all intents the frontier for another five hundred miles, forbade vessels to enter the lakes, or indeed to penetrate beyond Montreal, from the sea.

Naval stations were therefore essential upon the lakes themselves; and, since the Falls of Niagara closed the passage between Ontario and Erie, it was obvious that there must be at least one such station on each side of those falls. Even this was not all. The roads of that day were so bad as to be practically impassable except when frozen hard in winter; and therefore this same line of waters became the only means by which the supplies and stores of an army could be brought forward. Hence a chain of posts was essential to guard all narrow channels and to maintain communication between the more important stations, whether naval or commercial, which were studded along the waterway.

Let us now proceed to follow the lines of supply for both contending parties. If the Americans had had the foresight to build never so small a navy they might have harried our shipping on the ocean very seriously, and made the transport of troops and supplies most irksome; but being even more ignorant and foolish, if possible, than the English in all matters of war, they had neglected to make any such preparations and were powerless for grave mischief. Practically therefore there was free access from the British Isles across the Atlantic to Quebec, the key of Canada and the main base of the English operations. This was the only permanent fortification in the theatre of war; but, though it had been recently repaired and strengthened, it was in no condition to resist a vigorous and well-conducted siege.

The supreme importance of Quebec compelled the employment of a strong garrison to guard it; and consequently a full third of the regular force—twenty-four hundred rank and file—was there shut up. Nominally there were sixty thousand militia that could be called out for the defence of Lower Canada; but only two thousand of these had received any training, and the remainder were a mere mob; nor at the outset of the war were there more than four hundred spare muskets and twelve hundred thousand cartridges.

The first post above Quebec was Fort William Henry, about one hundred miles distant, at the junction of the Richelieu with the St. Lawrence. This was the most valuable station on the southern shore as a depot of stores and as a rendezvous for the shipping required for the defence of the St. Lawrence; and its value was the greater because there were several excellent defensive positions below it, where an enemy moving by either bank could be checked on the march to Quebec. It was therefore made proof against any sudden or irregular attack, and held by four companies of the Hundredth.

Fifty miles up the Richelieu and south of Fort William Henry was the frontier post of St. John at the head of the navigation of Lake Champlain, which was held by two companies as a place of observation only, the fortifications being in ruins and otherwise untenable. Halfway between these two was the supporting post of Chambly, which, being a place of assembly and a depot of arms for the militia, was occupied by three hundred irregulars and a detachment of the Royal Artillery, with two guns.

The last military station in Lower Canada was Montreal, the commercial capital, which was without any means of defence, its security depending on the maintenance of an impenetrable line between Chambly on the Richelieu and La Prairie on the St. Lawrence, together with an adequate flotilla upon both rivers. Here were stationed the Forty-Ninth Foot and a battery of light artillery. Twelve thousand militia were nominally at hand to aid in the defence, but, with the exception of six hundred under training, all were ill-armed and ill-disciplined.

Passing the boundary into Upper Canada, the first and most important post was Kingston, which commanded not only the head of the navigation of the St. Lawrence by boat, but also the communications between the two provinces. Moreover the Americans were in force on the opposite shore, with an excellent port, Sackett's Harbour, and a populous country at the back of it; whereas the Canadian militia at disposal did not exceed fifteen hundred men. It was therefore essential that Kingston, whose normal garrison was but four companies of Veterans, should be held in strength.

One hundred and fifty miles to west of Kingston on the northern shore stood York, the best situation in Upper Canada as a depot of stores and a naval base; but, when the war broke out, it was still unfortified, and the three companies of the Forty-First, which formed the garrison, had only fifteen hundred militia to back them. Then came a chain of small posts to guard the communications between Lakes Ontario and Erie: Fort George, a temporary work of little strength, Chippewa, and Fort Erie, which absorbed between them four or five companies. Over against them on the opposite side of the strait the Americans equally had their chain of posts, Forts Niagara and Schlosser, Black Rock, and Buffalo Creek.

Beyond, at the western end of Lake Erie, came Fort Amherstburg, the dockyard and marine arsenal for the Upper Lakes, defended by field-works, which had been recently repaired, and held by about one hundred and fifty regular infantry and artillery; the militia within call numbering about five hundred. The American counter-work to this was Fort Detroit on the other side of the strait which leads from Lake Erie to Lake Huron. Lastly, at the north-western head of Huron was a blockhouse enclosed by strong picquets on the island of St. Joseph's, which lies across the outlet from Lake Huron to Lake Superior. This was a mere place of assembly for Indians and was garrisoned by sixty or seventy infantry and artillery. On the outlet into Lake Michigan the British had no post, the Americans dominating the channel with the fort of Mackinac. (These details are drawn chiefly from Prevost's report on the defence of Canada. To Sec. of State, 18th May 1812).

To turn to the Americans, their first important objective would be Montreal, to which the old waterway by the Hudson, Lake George, and Lake Champlain led them by a direct and familiar line. Or, if they preferred to sever Upper from Lower Canada at Kingston, they had the alternative route by the Mohawk and Lake Oneida to Oswego on the south shore of Lake Ontario, and so by water to the principal naval base at Sackett's Harbour. Thus they enjoyed the enormous advantage of being able from their single base at Albany to strike the British line of communications at two vital points; and indeed if they managed their affairs with any energy, they might at the very outset compel the evacuation of Upper Canada and the withdrawal of all British troops to Kingston.

American naval superiority upon Lake Champlain, which should have been easy of attainment, was practically all that was required. In the most favourable circumstances the British could only hold Upper Canada with the help of the Indians; and, in spite of all the "dangerous delusive nonsense" talked during the American War of Independence about the employment of Indians by either side, it was now recognised that they could not be excluded from the struggle, and that, if they were not secured by the one party, they would assuredly be taken over by the other. The possession of Detroit and Mackinac to all intent assured the adherence of the Indians to the United States; and by way of the river Maumee the Americans had direct access to the western head of Lake Erie, from which they could, with naval superiority, either overwhelm the post of Amherstburg or take the British forts on the Niagara River in rear. The entire game, in fact, was in their hands; and they fully realised it. Jefferson wrote:

> The acquisition of Canada this year as far as the neighbourhood of Quebec, will be a mere matter of marching.

Let us now see what preparations the United States had made for this triumphant march. The establishment of the American Army in peace was ten thousand men, of which number there were in June 1812 nearly seven thousand upon the muster-rolls. Congress had authorised the levying of twenty-five thousand additional regular troops, making with engineers and artificers a nominal total of nearly thirty-seven thousand men. But of the new levies at that date not above five thousand recruits had been enlisted; the whole of these troops were of inferior quality, and their officers were not much better than themselves. Of militia the United States had of course a boundless quantity, of which one hundred thousand had been summoned by the President in April; but, as they could only be called out for terms of three months at the most, it was useless to look to them for prolonged work in the field. The country therefore fell back, in true English fashion, upon volunteers, whom the President was authorised, subject to the approval of the volunteers themselves, to organise upon the model of the Regular Army and to provide with officers.

As to commanders the American Government relied upon veterans of the War of Independence, selecting them rather for political than military reasons, and therefore appointing as senior general James Dearborn, and among the brigadiers William Hull, neither of whom had given a thought to military affairs for thirty years. As far as naval matters were concerned, the United States possessed a small corps of highly efficient officers; but so little had the true meaning of the war been realised that alike on Lake Erie, on Lake Ontario, and on Lake Champlain, the British naval force, though insignificant, was superior.

For on the British side, though not in the highest place, there was, what was lacking to the Americans, a man. The governor of Lower Canada and the commander-in-chief of the whole colony was Sir George Prevost, whom was at Dominica in 1805 and at Martinique in 1809, a good and skilful soldier, and still under fifty years of age. The first task set to him had been the choice of a civil administrator and commander-in-chief for Upper Canada, and he had made the excellent appointment of Brigadier-General Isaac Brock, late the commandant of the Forty-Ninth Foot.

A Guernseyman by birth, Brock had seen service first in North Holland in 1799, and then with Nelson at Copenhagen; and in 1802 he had sailed with his regiment for Canada, where he had visited all the military posts and thoroughly grasped the military situation. In 1806 he had succeeded for a time to the supreme command of the troops in both provinces, and had seized the opportunity to effect various reforms. First and foremost he had placed all marine business in the hands of the quartermaster-general's department, in default of a proper naval authority, and had issued orders that at every station a certain number of boats should be kept ready for instant service. It was therefore by his forethought that the British possessed naval supremacy upon the lakes in 1812.

In 1807, anticipating war in consequence of the affray between the *Leopard* and the *Chesapeake*, he repaired the fortifications of Quebec. Upon the arrival of Sir James Craig in October 1807 he remained as second in command of the troops in Lower Canada, and was thus able to superintend his improvements, until in 1810 he was transferred to the command of the Upper Province, to be ultimately established, as we have seen, as civil administrator also, with headquarters at York. His appointment, added to the despatch of the Forty-First to Upper Canada, produced the best results.

The inhabitants, who had thought that they were going to be abandoned, came forward with eager professions of loyalty and readiness to fight, while the Indians also showed an excellent spirit. It was then, in December 1811, that Brock wrote to Prevost, urging him to permit larger concentration of regular troops at so remote a spot as Amherstburg, in order to seize Detroit and Mackinac by surprise. The acquisition of these two posts would, as he pointed out, secure the friendship of the Indians, whose enmity to the United States would make a diversion upon the western frontier, and compel a respectable part of the American force to be distracted to that quarter.

For the rest, as he correctly divined, the main onslaught of the Americans would be directed towards the straits of Niagara, all other operations being subordinate to this principal attack; and it would therefore be necessary to bring additional regular troops to that point also, so as to hearten the militia. But unless Detroit and Mackinac were mastered at once, there was no alternative but to evacuate the whole country as far as Kingston. (Brock to Prevost, 2nd Dec. 1811; 12th Feb. 1812; Tapper's *Life of Brock*).

Prevost for his part was by no means disinclined to take the offensive; but his means were limited, and he had little hope of reinforcements from England, so that he did not feel justified in sending Brock more than three to four hundred extra regular troops. Prevost's position was a delicate one, for his predecessor had ruffled the susceptibilities of the Colonists, and though he was on the way to conciliate them, he had not yet had time to gain their confidence completely. However, the insolent speeches of the American orators had roused the pride of the Canadians; and the Parliament of Lower Canada after some demur consented to allow two thousand men to be balloted to serve for three months in two successive years.

In Upper Canada also Brock was able to carry a supplementary Militia Bill, and to secure the services of the flank-companies of the militia, which enabled him to embody and train from six to seven hundred men at once, with the expectation of thrice that number later on. The Glengarry Fencibles were likewise augmented to six hundred men, with every promise of becoming an excellent battalion; but even so the force at disposal was pitiably small, while the news of American preparations and of their tampering with the Indians became daily more ominous. To make matters worse, the latest instructions received from England gave notice that the exigencies of the service in Europe compelled the reduction of all foreign garrisons, and that two much weaker battalions would shortly arrive to take the place of the Forty-First and Forty-Ninth.

Above all, money was scarce; the government in England had warned Prevost that they could provide none; and it was certain that the declaration of war would definitely stop all advent of specie, the only source of supply being the United States. Altogether the situation of the governor was by no means enviable. (Sec. of State to Prevost, 2nd April, 15th May 1812).

By a singular piece of neglect Mr. Foster, the British Minister at Washington, sent no intelligence of the declaration of war to Upper Canada; and the news first reached both Brock and Prevost from private sources on the 24th of June. At that moment Brock had under his hand a force of some seventeen hundred of all ranks, (see list following), scattered about over a line of six to seven hundred miles from Kingston to St. Joseph's.

41st	900
10th Veterans	250
Newfoundland Fencibles	250
Royal Artillery	50
Provincial Seamen	50
rank and file	1500

His first step was to transport two companies of the Forty-First at once from York to the frontier at Niagara, and to follow them himself in an open boat to Fort George, where he established his headquarters. He was painfully embarrassed by the want of definite instructions from Prevost; but on the 28th of June he despatched orders to Captain Roberts, the commandant at St. Joseph's, to do his best to capture Mackinac. As it happened, Roberts received on the same day a communication from Prevost, bidding him try his utmost to secure his post, but in case of necessity to retreat.

Between these contradictory directions Roberts rightly chose those of Brock; and on the 16th of July he embarked a small force of about two hundred and twenty Europeans and four hundred Indians, with two light cannon, landed before Mackinac at dawn of the

17th, and by ten o'clock had placed one of his guns upon a height commanding the fort. Thereupon the American garrison, which had been left at the ridiculous strength of sixty men, surrendered without resistance.

Meanwhile the American General Hull had on the 30th of June reached the Maumee with one regiment of regular troops and some militia, making up a total altogether of about twenty-four hundred of all ranks. Here, being still unapprised of the declaration of war, he loaded a schooner with military stores, and having placed in her also his private papers, sent her down the river to Detroit. She was promptly captured by an English vessel from Amherstburg; and Hull's papers presently reached Brock at Fort St. George, giving him for the first time a true idea of his adversary's strength, which greatly exceeded his expectations.

On the 2nd of July Hull was apprised of the declaration of war, and a few days later he arrived at Detroit, where he received discretionary orders to capture Amherstburg. Accordingly on the 12th he crossed the strait, absolutely without molestation, and occupied the village of Sandwich, where he issued a pompous proclamation, offering protection to all who wished to escape from the tyranny of British rule and threatening death to every white man taken fighting in alliance with Indians. Such good fortune as the passage of the straits without so much as the firing of a shot would have encouraged any man of energy to storm Amherstburg out of hand. The Canadian militia as a matter of fact had behaved very ill. Many of them had dispersed to their homes; the remainder, fewer than five hundred, were utterly useless; and in fact the only men of value in the post were three hundred of the Forty-First. (Prevost to Sec. of State, 30th July 1812).

But Hull mistrusted himself and his troops; and after two days' hesitation he called a council of war, which as usual resolved not to fight. Thereupon he sat still at Sandwich to await the arrival of siege-artillery.

The news of the occupation of Sandwich reached Brock on the 20th of July, and threw him into the greatest anxiety. An American force, which he reckoned at twelve hundred strong, lay in his front, and was in itself nothing very formidable; but he thought it incredible that Hull should not have mastered Amherstburg, and he dreaded not only the general effect of such a disaster upon the inhabitants, but also the probable arrival of a thousand men of Hull's force in his rear. However, he sent Colonel Proctor, an active officer, to take command at Amherstburg, though with great misgivings lest he should arrive too late; and despatched a small detachment of regulars and militia to check the raids of the Americans from Sandwich.

For the moment everything seemed to be going wrong. Prevost, suddenly making up his mind that the Americans would not take the offensive, deprecated any aggression on Brock's part lest thereby he should unite the two political parties in the States in common hostility against Canada.

A tribe of Indians, upon whose assistance Brock had counted, refused to join him; and, since this action was a direct menace to the inhabitants, he was obliged to leave the militia of one district to guard their homes instead of calling them out into the field. The militia of Norfolk county, either through disloyalty or because they were overawed by Hull's proclamation, refused to march; and one party of five hundred, farther to the west, actually sought the protection of the enemy.

Even the select flank-companies showed impatience to return to their own place. Brock was burning to take personal command at Amherstburg, but he was detained by the necessity of meeting the legislature at York on the 27th of July. He had hoped to obtain from it drastic powers for dealing with refractory militia; but honourable members had made up their minds that their country would soon be in the hands of the Americans, and refused to compromise themselves. Brock therefore prorogued them after eight days' session, having obtained from them at least some supplies. He had already been obliged to establish a paper currency; and the success of this measure together with the news of the fall of Mackinac, which reached him on the 29th, were his only consolations during this most melancholy time. (Tupper's *Life of Brock*).

Prevost also had not been without his troubles. Immediately that the declaration of war became known, some of the parishes about Montreal refused to furnish their quota of militia; and there ensued a regular riot, in the course of which a body of insurgents marched off to seize the king's boats which were lying at La Chine. A few shots from a company of the Forty-Ninth soon dispersed them with a loss of one man killed and another wounded; and this timely severity quickly brought about complete submission. Eight thousand men were presently embodied, and the arrival on the 15th of July of the Hundred and Third Regiment at Quebec helped to restore confidence not a little.

But Sir George still hesitated to detach any reinforcements to

Brock until the 25th, and then he sent only one hundred and fifty Fencibles and Veterans, to strengthen the garrison of Kingston and release a company of the Forty-Ninth for service with Brock's handful of men. Herein Prevost showed want of energy and enterprise.

It is true that the Americans were forming depots and building *bateaux* on Lake Champlain, but they had little appearance of strength; and an enemy which had reached no more advanced stage than this three weeks after the commencement of hostilities, was not greatly to be dreaded. Moreover, Prevost was daily expecting another British battalion, the Royal Scots, at Quebec; and though this corps had been sent out only in the way of a relief and not as a reinforcement, he could perfectly well take the responsibility of retaining it. His chief staff officer, Colonel Baynes, pressed him earnestly to despatch further troops to Brock, but in vain. (*Life of Brock*).

The truth seems to be that the general, in spite of all warnings, persisted in his belief that the internal divisions of America would avert any serious operation of the enemy; and on the 29th of July a report reached him which tended greatly to fortify him in his opinion.

By a singular coincidence, on the very day that the United States had declared war the British Government had revoked the obnoxious Orders in Council, so far as concerned America; and Ministers therefore hoped that, in spite of all that had passed, friendly relations might be maintained. On the 1st of August Prevost received official confirmation of the news, and at once sent Colonel Baynes to treat with General Dearborn for a suspension of hostilities. Dearborn, who was at Albany, consented to confine his troops to the defensive until instructions should arrive from his government; but he gave no orders to Hull, whom, as he afterwards explained, he did not consider to be under his command.

Indeed it was certain, from the distances to be traversed, that intelligence of the agreement could not reach either Hull or Brock for at least two or three weeks. Prevost has been greatly blamed for proposing this armistice which, as shall be seen, produced very mischievous consequences; and yet in doing so he was unquestionably fulfilling the wishes of the British Cabinet. So far, he had received no instructions from Downing Street subsequent to the opening of hostilities; but all despatches previous to it had impressed upon him the fact that neither men nor money could be spared for Canada from home, that every possible soldier was required for service in Europe, even to the weakening of colonial garrisons, and that all care must be taken not to irritate the United States.

Indeed the British Government, as is proved by the despatches of the Secretary of State, made sure that the repeal of the Orders in Council would restore amity between the two nations; and Prevost's action in seeking to build up peace upon such a repeal was not only approved but applauded. (Sec. of State to Prevost, 2nd April, 15th May, 1st, 10th Aug., 1st Oct. 1812).

Beyond doubt also Liverpool and his colleagues were right in endeavouring to avoid an American war, for they had enemies enough upon their hands already; and Prevost, who was very far from an unintelligent man, may be said to have shown high moral courage of a kind in subordinating his own plans and desires to the yet higher interests of the empire. Moreover, Mr. Foster, our late Minister at Washington, had impressed upon Prevost the fact that, unless the territory of the United States were invaded, the American Government could not order the militia to pass beyond its own frontier.

Altogether there would have been very much to be said for the maintenance of a pacific attitude, but for two principal facts: the first, that the British Government did not realise the actual situation in America; the second, that the only possible means of defending Canada was by a brisk offensive. To sit still was simply to give the Americans time to prepare an overwhelming force; and it was idle to contend, as Prevost did, that the divisions among the Americans would be healed by British aggression and best kept open by an ostentatious inoffensive. Nothing breeds recrimination so surely as failure.

However there was no obstacle to prevent Prevost from sending money, reinforcements, and stores to Brock, which he eventually did on the 13th; and meanwhile that indefatigable officer, happily ignorant of all armistices, had collected two hundred and fifty militia and passed over with them from York to Burlington Bay, whence he marched by land to Long Point. Here he embarked his men and sixty of the Forty-First in every description of open boat that he could obtain from the settlers on the shore, and set off on the voyage of two hundred miles to Amherstburg.

At the best of times such a journey would have been perilous, for the coast in many places consists of lofty cliffs with never a creek for shelter; and the flotilla encountered heavy rain and tempestuous weather. Once Brock's own boat ran upon a sunken rock and could not be shoved off till the general set the example of jumping overboard, when everyone with him did likewise and soon set the craft afloat again. Animated by his infectious activity the little squadron was by great exertion brought to Amherstburg shortly before midnight on the 13th, the militia having endured the extreme fatigue and hardship of the journey with a constancy and cheerfulness beyond all praise. Here he found that Proctor had not been idle, having sent out small parties to harass Hull's communications, upon the whole with considerable success and very slight loss.

It was encouraging also to find that letters from Hull, most despondent in tone, had been intercepted. In fact on the 7th and 8th of August the American general had withdrawn his troops to the American side of the strait, leaving at first from two to three hundred men entrenched on the British side, but recalling them also before they could be cut off. Altogether the outlook was not unpromising for such a leader as Brock.

His first act was to assemble the Indians under their very remarkable leader Tecumseh, and tell them that he was come to ask their assistance in driving the enemy from Detroit, and to learn from them how to make war in the forest. "Hoooh . . . this is a man!" ejaculated Tecumseh as he listened; and the plan of attack was soon agreed upon. Batteries for five guns and mortars were constructed against Fort Detroit; and having sent to Hull a summons, which was defied, on the evening of the 15th, Brock despatched six hundred Indians under a British officer across the strait in the night, with orders to take up a position to cover the landing of the troops in the morning.

At six o'clock on the 16th the batteries opened fire, and three hundred and thirty regular troops, (R.A., 30; 41st, 250; Newfoundland Rgt. 50), with five light guns and four hundred militia crossed the water and disembarked without molestation from four to five miles below and west of Detroit.

By all accounts Hull's force numbered at least two thousand men; and Brock's intention had consequently been to take up a strong position close to the fort, so as to compel the enemy to come out and fight him; but upon landing he heard that Hull had detached a party of five hundred men under Colonel M'Arthur three days before, and that these were on the point of returning. He decided therefore to attack at once, and moved forward upon Detroit, having his right covered by the armed vessel *Queen Charlotte* and his left by the Indians, who moved through the skirts of the forest.

As he advanced, the Americans abandoned a commanding eminence, which they had strengthened by palisades and by two heavy

TECUMSEH

guns, and retired into the fort; and, before Brock could form his columns of assault, a white flag came out to suggest a capitulation. It was very soon agreed that Detroit should be surrendered and that the entire American force, including M'Arthur's detachment, should become prisoners; and at noon Brock marched into the fort at the head of his troops. A brig of war, thirty-three pieces of ordnance, and a considerable quantity of munitions fell into the hands of the British; and Brock reckoned the number of the captured at not fewer than two thousand five hundred men.

It is difficult to account for this extraordinary behaviour on the part of Hull. His troops, it is true, were bad and undisciplined, and the fort was encumbered by a number of quivering refugees who had been considerably agitated by the cannonade from the other side of the strait; but he had nearly a month's supplies with plenty of ammunition; and reinforcements to the number of nearly five thousand men were within a few days' march of him. More remarkable still, on his arrival at Montreal he showed no sense of shame or humiliation, being content to rail upon the government at Washington and lay all responsibility for the disaster to their charge.

Indeed he was not above uttering the falsehood that he had not one day's powder left at Detroit, and evinced no embarrassment when confronted with the return of the ample store surrendered with the fort. (Hull's bearing at Montreal, *Life of Brock*). Thinking that his murmurings might be useful in heightening the discontent of the Americans with their government, Prevost allowed him to go on parole to Boston, where no doubt his story gained for him some credit with political partisans, but can hardly have won sympathy from honest men.

Two years later he was tried by a court-martial, which very properly found him guilty of cowardice and condemned him to death, though the sentence was remitted in consideration of his services in the War of Independence. It may be urged that the idea of sending an expedition against Amherstburg at all was wrong, since the place must have fallen of itself upon the capture of the British posts at Niagara or at the mouth of the St. Lawrence, and that in any case such an enterprise, without naval superiority first secured on Lake Erie, was absurd. The rulers of America in their ineffable conceit ignored all military considerations, thinking that their armed rabble had only to walk over the Canadian border and seize what it pleased; and no terms of contempt and condemnation can be too strong for them. But a military commander has a duty to his country as well as to his government.

It is his business to endeavour to make good the mistakes of his masters, not to aggravate their blunders by his own misconduct, and then to take the lead in reviling those that are set in authority over him. In fact Hull's conduct was infamous, and he was very lucky to escape hanging.

However, the immediate effect of this affair naturally was to depress the Americans profoundly, while inspiring the Canadian militia with confidence, overawing the disaffected and heartening the loyal throughout the length and breadth of the country. Brock, fully realising this, flew back to Niagara as soon as he had arranged affairs at Detroit, but was met on the 23rd of August, while sailing across Lake Erie, with the news of the armistice concluded by Prevost with Dearborn. The tidings filled him with mortification and dismay, for he had laid all his plans for attacking the American naval arsenal at Sackett's Harbour, and there can be little doubt that he would have succeeded; in which case the enemy's task of overthrowing the British naval superiority on Lake Ontario would have been rendered infinitely more difficult.

Moreover it naturally enraged him to see that naval superiority made worthless by the armistice, and supplies and stores, of which the enemy was greatly in need, travelling comfortably by water to Niagara to strengthen the force which he would ultimately have to combat. However he was fain to return to Fort George and await events. On the 30th of Aug. an *aide-de-camp* arrived at Montreal with a letter from Dearborn reporting that the government at Washington declined to suspend hostilities, though adding an expression of his own ardent wish that an honourable and permanent peace might shortly be concluded. Prevost's letter carrying the intelligence to Brock reached that officer on the 4th of September at Kingston, to which he was paying a flying visit, and decided him to return to Fort George immediately.

He found the enemy's numbers at Niagara so greatly increased and their demeanour so menacing that he applied to Sir George on the 7th for further reinforcements; and it was at this period that the relations between the two officers began to grow strained. Prevost, notwithstanding the expiration of the armistice, had given positive orders to Brock to stand on the defensive; and, on receiving the latter's request for additional troops, he answered very curtly that, unless the attitude of the Americans at Niagara became less threatening, Detroit must be evacuated and the garrison at Amherstburg reduced.

Brock meanwhile, upon intelligence that the Americans were again advancing upon Amherstburg, had actually determined not only not to reduce the garrison but even to reinforce it; and he declined, under Prevost's discretionary instructions, to evacuate Detroit. The effect of such a measure, he said, would be that the Indians would either exterminate the population on the American side of the strait, or make terms with the enemy against the British. The policies of the two men were in fact radically opposed to each other. Prevost not only believed in the inoffensive as the path to peace, but at heart was evidently for abandoning everything west of Niagara, if not indeed Kingston.

According to the ordinary rules of war he was upon the latter point undoubtedly right; for the effort to hold too many posts may mean the loss of all. Brock, on the other hand, recognised the Americans for what they were, a vindictive, but unmilitary and unready nation, with whom at the outset every kind of liberty could be taken, and whose folly should be turned to the utmost advantage before adversity should convert it into wisdom. (For correspondence between Brock and Prevost, *Life of Brock*. One letter of Brock, dated 7th Sept., is missing; but its purport is given in Prevost to Sec. of State, 12th Sept. 1812).

Unfortunately the American Government had in one respect found wisdom early, for on the 3rd of September they had ordered Captain Isaac Chauncey, at that time employed in the navy-yard at New York, to take the naval command on Lakes Erie and Ontario and "use every exertion to obtain control of them this fall." On the latter lake there was already the Oneida, a brig of eighteen guns, manned by officers and men of the United States Navy. Upon Erie there was no naval force of any kind; wherefore Chauncey almost immediately despatched Lieutenant Elliott to select a site for a naval yard and to contract for the construction of two vessels of three hundred tons apiece. Meanwhile he toiled with extraordinary energy to send forward everything that was requisite for a naval station, including over one hundred guns with their ammunition, one hundred and forty ship's carpenters, and seven hundred seamen and marines.

Nothing was ready excepting the guns; every carriage required to be constructed and every shot to be cast; so hopelessly ignorant were the rulers of the United States of the meaning of war. All this mass of material was sent by water to Albany; and on the 26th of September Chauncey himself started up the Hudson in a steamer, and made his way thence by land to Sackett's Harbour. So bad were the roads that he was obliged to order all stores to be sent by way of Lake Oneida to Oswego, notwithstanding the many breaks in the water-way and the danger from English ships in the passage from Oswego to Sackett's Harbour. Elliott, who had reached Buffalo on the 14th of September, reported that in that quarter also there were long stretches of road so infamous that no ordnance could be taken over them until deep snow should permit the use of sledges. In fact it was hopeless to think of making any naval effort upon Lake Erie until the following year, and Chauncey had no choice but to resign himself to the inevitable.

Happy chance, however, gave him the advantage for which he had not dared to hope. On the 8th of October there anchored before Port Erie the *Caledonia*, which so far had given the British supremacy on the lake, and the *Detroit*, which had been surrendered by Hull under the capitulation. Both were commanded and manned, as indeed were all the British vessels, by Canadians, who, through no fault of their own, were very far from efficient.

It was, as Prevost complained, one of his principal difficulties to find suitable officers and crews for his ships. Sailors were scraped together wherever they could be found, and were eked out with Newfoundland Fencibles, as most likely to be familiar with the sea; but the officers to train these men were wanting, the colonial commanders having neither experience nor energy. By chance the first detachment of ninety seamen from New York was within call of Buffalo, and Elliott sent orders to hurry them forward.

At noon of the 8th they arrived; and at one o'clock on the following morning Elliott embarked with one hundred sailors and soldiers, who, after two hours hard pulling against the stream, came alongside the two vessels by surprise, and mastered them without difficulty. The *Detroit* and *Caledonia* carried sixty-eight men only, and were encumbered by forty American prisoners from Amherstburg; but even so their capture was very disgraceful. Elliott succeeded in carrying off the *Caledonia*, but the British batteries compelled him to run the *Detroit* aground on the American shore and abandon her. The British then boarded her, but being unable to warp her off from want of an anchor, and being also not a little galled by the American musketry, in their turn deserted her; whereupon the Americans put an end to the matter by setting her on fire. Elliott's blow, boldly and skilfully aimed, had struck home indeed.

Brock was deeply chagrined, he wrote to Prevost:

25

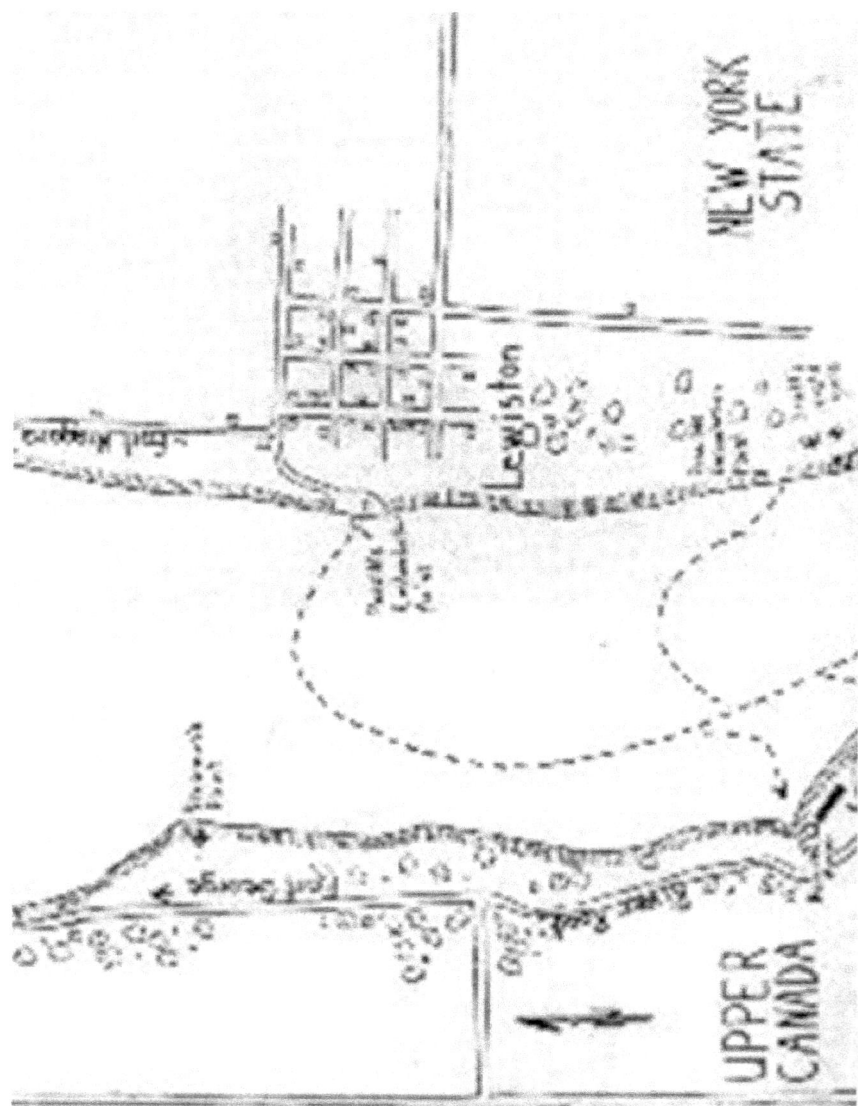

Niagara River

Lewiston

NEW YORK STATE

UPPER CANADA

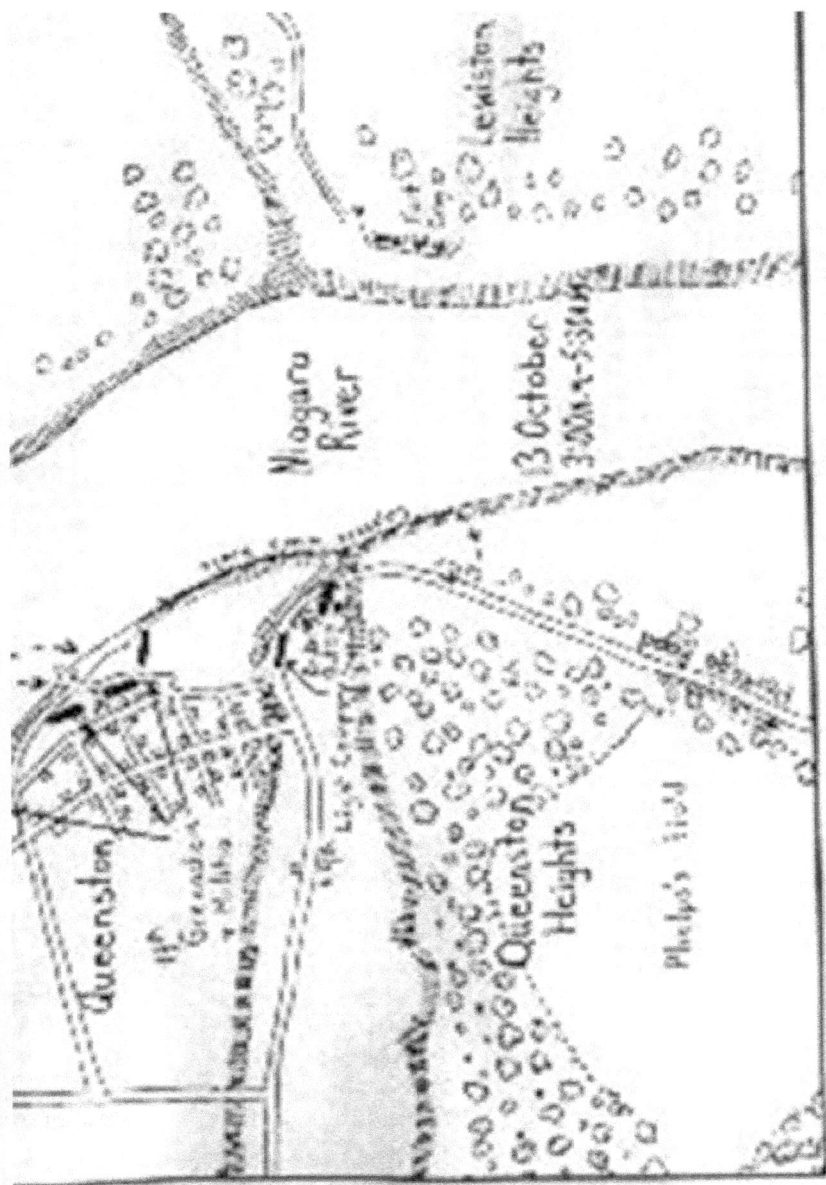

Lewiston Heights

Niagara River

13 October 3:00 a.m.–5:30 a.m.

Queenston

Mr. Grundy's Mills

Queenston Heights

Phelps' Farm

This event may reduce us to incalculable distress. The enemy is making every exertion to gain a naval superiority upon both lakes, which if they accomplish I do not see how we can retain the country. More vessels are fitting out for war on the other side of Squaw Island (the naval station selected by Elliott) which I should have attempted to destroy but for Your Excellency's repeated instructions to forbear. Now such a force is collected for their protection as will render every operation against them very hazardous.—Brock to Prevost, 11th Oct. 1812. Tupper.

This tacit reproach to Prevost for tying his hands may be excused, as the mischief was irreparable. The loss of the cargo alone was serious, for it included four cannon and two hundred muskets, which were none too plentiful; but the loss of the ship was beyond estimation. Brock had intended to despatch reinforcements and supplies to Amherstburg, but he was now compelled to send the men only in his one remaining ship, the *Lady Prevost*, and to direct her to return as soon as possible for the victuals. He declined, however, to subject Proctor to the restrictions imposed upon himself, and his last orders to him were "to keep the enemy in a state of constant ferment" by every description of harassing attack.

Meanwhile the American Army on the other side of the strait had grown until it had reached a total of some eight thousand men. Rather over fourteen hundred regular troops were stationed on the extreme right at Fort Niagara and at Four Mile Creek, about three miles in rear of it; and at Lewiston, six miles to the south, were rather more than three thousand men, over two-thirds of them New York militia and the remainder regular infantry. The whole of these were under the command of Major-General Rensselaer, but he, being only a militiaman, wisely trusted for counsel to his adjutant-general, who was also his cousin bearing the same name, and a colonel in the Regular Army. South of the falls about Buffalo were over sixteen hundred regulars, four hundred militia, and two hundred and fifty sailors under Brigadier Smyth, a professional officer, nominally under Van Rensselaer's command, but highly disinclined to work with him.

To oppose this force Brock had six companies of the Forty-Ninth, four or five of the Forty-First and a handful of artillery, perhaps eight hundred regular troops altogether, besides some four hundred militia and two to three hundred Indians; the whole being necessarily dispersed along the front of thirty-six miles from his headquarters at Fort George to Fort Erie. At Fort George itself were stationed the detachment of the Forty-First, some four hundred strong, about one hundred militia and two to three score Indians. At Vrooman's or Scott's Point, about a mile to south, was a twenty-four-pounder gun, mounted *en barbette* to command the river, under the charge of a detachment of militia; and two miles above it at Brown's Point were two more companies of militia.

Three miles to south of Brown's Point stood the village of Queenston, consisting then of about twenty houses with gardens and orchards, of a barrack, and of a large stone building. At this point the ground rises abruptly to a height of three hundred and fifty feet above the water; and immediately above Queenston the banks of the river become cliffs. About half-way up this ascent was mounted an eighteen-pounder, the care of which, together with that of the village on the bank of the river, was committed to the flank companies of the Forty-Ninth and a company of militia. The remainder of the British force was at Chippewa and Fort Erie; but Brock had concentrated his principal strength at the northern end of the strait, suspecting that the large detachment of the enemy at Four Mile Creek portended an attempt upon Fort George.

For some time past the American militiamen at Lewiston had amused themselves by firing across the river—just at that point little more than two hundred yards broad—at all passers-by and at the windows of the houses. Roused by the bold exploit of Elliott these heroes informed their chief that he must lead them to the attack, otherwise they would go home, a proceeding thoroughly characteristic of amateur soldiers of all nations, who imagine that war is a matter of fighting and, if possible, of pillage, rather than of self-denial and endurance. Rensselaer laid his plans to surprise the British at daybreak of the 11th; but, the gentleman in charge of the flotilla having disappeared very early in the proceedings, the attempt was abandoned.

Unfortunately for the American general a British officer with a flag of truce landed on the same evening on the eastern shore, observed the number of boats concealed among the rocks, and drew his own conclusions. Ignorant of this fact, Rensselaer decided to repeat his attack on the 13th. A battery of four heavy pieces and two field-guns had been established above Lewiston to protect the passage and to play upon the British post at Queenston; and it was arranged that three hundred regulars and as many militia should be the first to cross the river under the fire of these cannon.

Fourteen boats only were to hand, two of which would carry eighty men apiece, and the remainder thirty only; but it was hoped that the advanced party would suffice to obtain a footing on the Canadian shore, after which the craft would return and bring reinforcements to the number, if necessary, of over three thousand men.

The night was pitch dark and slight rain was falling when the boats shoved off. Three, including the two largest, were carried down stream by the current, very rapid at that short distance below the falls, and the smallest of the three alone landed its freight some way below Queenston, the two others reverting to their starting-point. Ten only reached the landing-place at Queenston safely; the troops disembarked and formed; and the boats put back at once to bring over more men. But meanwhile the guard which held Queenston, consisting of about one hundred men of the Forty-Ninth and some militia under Captain Dennis, had turned out and saluted the invaders with a destructive volley, which sent them flying behind the rocks for cover. Colonel van Rensselaer, who was in command, was wounded in four places, and the casualties are said to have numbered over fifty, which is probably no exaggeration, for the range was short and the British fired low. (Van Rensselaer's wounds were all below the waist).

The boats were slow in returning, and, as they came, two of them were again carried down-stream, the one below Queenston and the other to Vrooman's battery where both parties were taken prisoners. At the same time the American cannon opened a vague fire in the dark, which roused Brock from his sleep at Fort George. The remainder of the two companies under Dennis's command quietly joined their leader at the sound of the cannonade; and the rest of the garrison of Queenston under Captain Williams took post at the battery higher up the hill.

Soon afterwards Brock came galloping up, alone and unattended, as fast as his horse could carry him. On his way he was met by a subaltern of the detachment of militia at Brown's Point, who, hastening to his side, received his orders to summon the reserve from Fort George, and to send out a party of Indians to cover their right flank as they advanced. Turning up the hill short of Queenston, Brock made straight for the eighteen-pounder battery, where observing that the Americans, who had been reinforced, were beginning to press upon Dennis, he sent Williams down to join him, reserving only twelve men for the protection of the gun.

Suddenly this small detachment was startled by a volley of musketry on its left flank. Colonel van Rensselaer, in spite of his wounds, had instructed his second in command, Captain Wool, to move along the shore northward where there was a fisherman's path leading up the heights which, for some reason, had been left unguarded. By this path Wool ascended the hill with an advanced party of sixty men, coming with such suddenness upon Brock's little band that the general could not attempt even to remount, but was fain to rush down to the foot of the hill. Here he recalled Williams's detachment and led it up the hill to retake the battery; the militia from Brown's Point being now near at hand to support him.

The ascent was covered with patches of scrub from which the American riflemen poured in a very deadly fire; and Wool had by this time been reinforced to a strength of some five hundred men. None the less Brock drove back the first detachment of one hundred and fifty troops; and, although Wool strengthened his fighting line, the British continued to gain ground until the Americans were forced to the edge of the cliffs.

Here some of the enemy hoisted the white flag; but Wool tore it down; and at this critical moment Brock was struck by a bullet in the right breast, and in a few minutes was dead. His last words were "Push on the York Volunteers"—meaning thereby the detachment at Brown's Point, which now came up under the command of the attorney general, a most gallant gentleman by name John Macdonell. Rallying the few men left of Williams's company, for Williams himself had also been disabled, Macdonell led his little band again to the charge. He had apparently just recovered the battery when he was shot dead, whereupon the whole of his party gave way and dispersed. Dennis, who had maintained a stubborn fight from house to house until at last driven from the village by the American heavy guns, saw the hopelessness of attempting to regain the heights against superior numbers. He therefore fell back towards Queenston, leaving Brock's body covered with a blanket in the village.

It was now ten o'clock. The Americans had gained their object, though with difficulty, thanks chiefly to the bravery of Colonel van Rensselaer and the stubborn courage of Wool who, albeit himself wounded, had by great exertions contrived to make his men stand. They had now nearly a thousand men on the Canadian shore, and General van Rensselaer crossed over to join them with his chief engineer, in order to lay out an entrenched camp; sending orders at the same time for additional reinforcements to come to him immediately.

THE BATTLE OF
QUEENSTON HEIGHTS
13 October 1812
(AFTER CRUIKSHANK)

0   ¼   ½

Scale in Miles

N

Route of General Sheaffe's T

To St. Davids

PLATEAU (175' above River)

QUEENSTON HEIGHTS (340' above F

Detachment from Chippawa

Road

Durham's House •

To Fort George

Vrooman's Point

Troops

R I V E R →

Village of
LEWISTON

Landing

Hamilton House

Village of
QUEENSTON
(70' above River)

Landing

Battery →

U N I T E D

N I A G A R A

Barrack

river)

→ British

American Forces

Fort Gra

LEWISTON
HEIGHTS

S T A T E S

to Niagara Falls

c

QUEENSTON 1812

Brigadier Smyth, however, declined to send any of his troops; and the American militiamen, who a few hours before had been so clamorous for the offensive, now stood upon their constitutional rights and refused to move out of their own territory. They had seen a boat sunk by a shot from the British cannonade at Vrooman's point, and had not relished the spectacle.

The general recrossed the water to exhort them to come on, but in vain. Some hours passed, and at two o'clock the reserve from Fort George under Colonel Sheaffe of the Forty-Ninth came upon the scene. Guided by Brock's orders to cover his right flank with a body of Indians, Sheaffe struck westward just before reaching Queenston, leaving a small party of infantry and two guns under Captain Holcroft of the artillery close to the village, in order to menace the passage of the river.

He then fetched a wide compass through the forest, ascended the heights about a mile and a half from the river and came down upon the rear of the Americans with his front nearly parallel to the water. His force, by the junction of Dennis's detachment and of another small reinforcement from Chippewa, amounted by this time to nearly one thousand white troops, fully half of them regulars, besides over two hundred Indians; and he had with him two light guns. The Americans on the Canadian bank were nearly as numerous, but appear to have been scattered, so that the force actually opposed to Sheaffe was greatly inferior to his own in numbers, and had but one gun. These faced about to receive the attack; but they were caught in a trap, and they knew it.

Their only line of retreat lay down the very steep hill northward to Queenston, in which case they would be exposed to the fire of Holcroft's guns and to the rush of the British and Indians upon their flank; and all other access to the river was barred for fully six miles by cliffs. Sheaffe came down upon them at once, apparently edging them steadily to southward, so as to coop them up beyond hope of salvation, while Holcroft's guns effectually prevented any attempt of American troops to pass the river. A volley or two and a charge with the bayonet sufficed to decide the issue.

The Americans fled in panic, many of them jumping over the cliffs in their terror; and presently the whole of them surrendered. When the full tale of prisoners was made up, it was found to amount to nine hundred and twenty-five, while the number of killed, wounded and drowned was reckoned at three hundred more. The British casualties

DETROIT 1811

did not exceed ninety-four killed, wounded and missing, of whom forty-seven belonged to the flank companies of the Forty-Ninth; but the disparity of loss was a sorry compensation for the death of Brock. (*Life of Brock*, Richardson's *War of 1812,* Lucas's *Canadian War of 1812,* Kingsford's *History of Canada*, vol. viii., and Macdonell's *Glengarry in Canada*.).

Now was the time for Sheaffe to push his advantage. Most of the captured Americans were regular troops; few except dismayed militiamen remained on the opposite shore; the chief adviser of the enemy's General was disabled; and all was panic and confusion. Fort Niagara was the one permanent fortress built of masonry on the border of Upper Canada, and in the course of the day its guns had plied Fort George with red-hot shot with considerable effect. There can be little doubt that it would have surrendered if threatened immediately; and its destruction, at any rate in Prevost's opinion, would not only have removed a cause of permanent anxiety and disquietude, but would have secured the Niagara River to the British until the close of the war.

Van Rensselaer, however, proposed an armistice for three days, which was weakly accepted by Sheaffe, and upon the expiry of that period was prolonged for an indefinite time, being made terminable upon thirty hours' notice from either side. This concession simply enabled the Americans to bring forward their reinforcements at their leisure, according to the false system vaguely inculcated from Downing Street, too readily adopted by Prevost, and too slavishly imitated by Sheaffe. General van Rensselaer presently resigned, making way for his former subordinate Smyth, who inaugurated his assumption of command by a proclamation reflecting upon the appointment of "popular men," such as Hull and his predecessor, to the leadership of armies. To prove himself better than they, he allowed the truce to continue until he had assembled over four thousand men about Black Rock, and had built and procured boats sufficient to carry thirty-five hundred men across the river; and then on the 19th of November he denounced the armistice.

He did not, however, move until the 28th, when in the first hours of the morning he sent about four hundred men across the river in two parties, the one to master a small British post about two miles from Fort Erie, the other to break down the bridge over Frenchmen's creek, and so to sever the communication between Fort Erie and the post at Chippewa. The details of what ensued are obscure. All that is certain is that British and American parties wandered up and down

37

the bank in the darkness, sometimes firing at each other, sometimes mistaking each other for friends; that the Americans for a time were masters of one British post and of three or four British guns, but that they were dispossessed by a superior force at daylight, when such of them as had not already recrossed the river were captured. The casualties on each side were about fifty killed and wounded and thirty to forty prisoners; but the results of the enterprise were absolutely nugatory.

Having announced that his men "would conquer or die," Smyth professed himself undaunted by this mishap. His next step was to parade his whole force on his own side of the river, and in view of its formidable appearance to invite the British commandant at Fort Erie to surrender, in order to "spare the effusion of blood." This offer being declined, the general formed the valorous resolution of crossing the river on the morning of the 30th, but then discovered that his officers also held strong opinions respecting the shedding of blood in general and of their own blood in particular, and were unwilling to expose the flotilla to the fire of the British batteries in broad daylight. Thereupon Smyth deferred the operation until the dark hours of the following morning; but, when daylight broke, only fifteen hundred men had been embarked, the rest being still on the shore and firmly resolved not to leave it.

Smyth therefore counter-ordered the movement, and announced that he would make no further attempt to invade Canada until reinforced, or, in other words, that he would undertake nothing further during the current season. Upon this his army broke into tumultuous demonstrations of delight, saluting the glad tidings with a wild and prolonged discharge of muskets; and so ended the campaign of 1812 at the frontier of Niagara. But for the death of Brock its conclusion would have been very different; and but for the thwarting of Brock's plans by Prevost the entire situation would have been transformed.

On the frontier of Lake Champlain the feebleness of Dearborn was almost as great as that of Smyth. He did not advance to Champlain until November, and even then accomplished no more than the surprise of a small post of militia; whereupon Prevost retaliated by the capture of an American block-house and its garrison. On the 22nd of November Dearborn put his men into winter quarters at Albany, Plattsburg, and Burlington, having made as inglorious a campaign as ever general did. Nor were the American attempts in the extreme west more fortunate. General Harrison, who had succeeded Hull, had advanced upon Detroit with some ten thousand men, whom, owing to the difficulties of transport and supply, he had divided into three columns. Of these the left-hand column of fifteen hundred men under General Winchester reached Fort Defiance at the junction of the Auglaize and Maumee Rivers towards the end of October; the centre column, which should have followed in the track taken by Hull, failed altogether to attain its appointed station; and the right-hand column under Harrison himself occupied Upper Sandusky towards the end of December; the united strength of the two columns being over six thousand men.

Impatient to strike a blow, Harrison ordered Winchester to descend the Maumee as far as the Rapids, ten or twelve miles from Lake Erie, and there prepare sleds for a swift advance upon Amherstburg and Detroit as soon as the lake should be frozen. Winchester arrived at the Rapids on the 10th of January 1813, where he presently received a message from a small settlement of French Canadians at Frenchtown, about thirty miles to north-east, begging him to drive away a party of three hundred militia and Indians which had occupied the village. He therefore detached a force of nearly seven hundred men under Colonel Lewis, who, after a severe march, great part of it on the ice of the Maumee, came upon Frenchtown on the afternoon of the 18th, and after a sharp action drove back the British party some sixteen miles to Brownstown. The retreat was most gallantly covered by the Indians, whose stubbornness cost the Americans sixty-seven killed and wounded, with slight loss to themselves.

On learning of this success Winchester proceeded at once with two hundred and fifty men to reinforce Lewis, while Harrison hastened with every man that he could spare to the rapids of the Maumee. Proctor at Amherstburg, being apprised early on the 19th of what had passed, likewise directed all the troops at his disposal to assemble at Brownstown. Advancing from thence with about five hundred whites, eight hundred Indians, and three light guns, he moved southward across the ice, and on the evening of the 21st bivouacked within five miles of the enemy's camp.

★★★★★★

Prevost gives Proctor's force as 3 cos. of the 41st, a detachment of the Newfoundland Fencibles, the sailors of the ship *Queen Charlotte*; 150 of the Essex Militia; in all not above 500 r. and f. (to Sec. of State, 8th Feb. 1813). Allowing for men left to hold the fort, we may take the number present in the action at 500

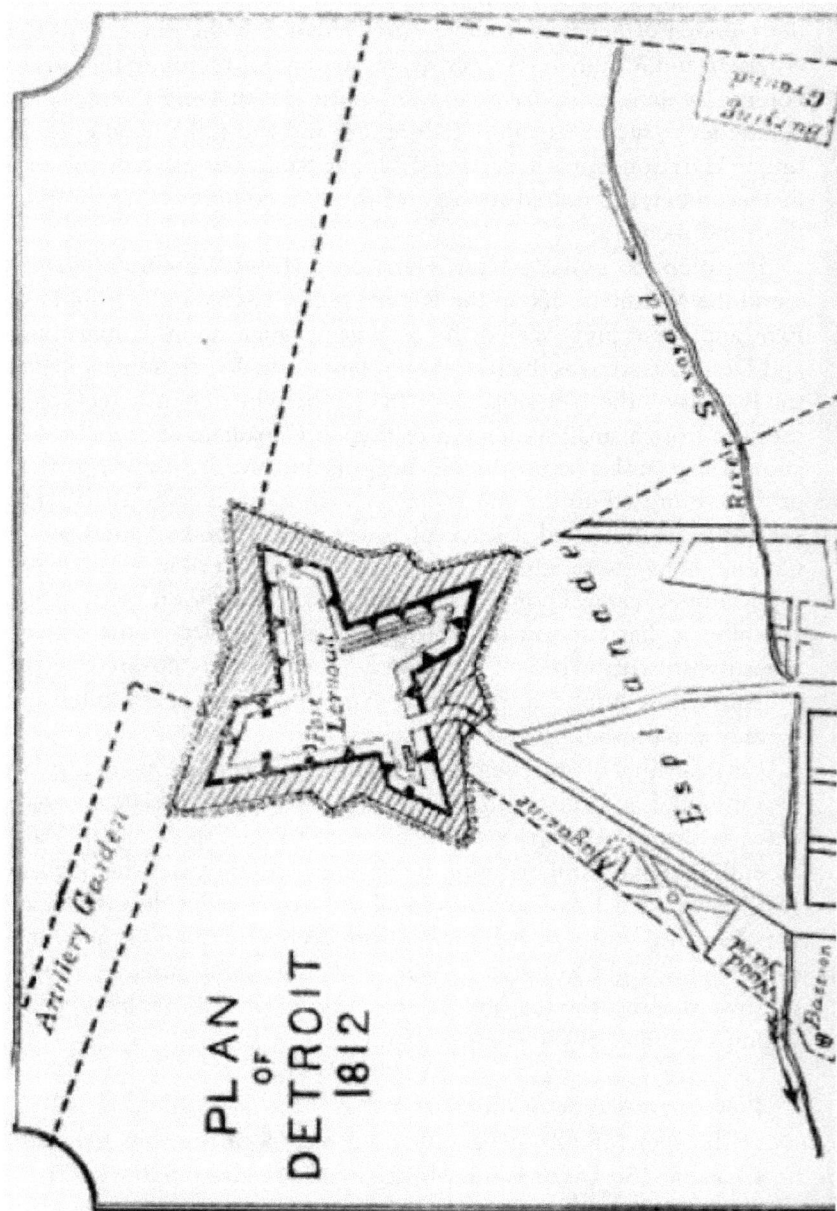

PLAN
OF
DETROIT
1812

Fort Lernoult

Artillery Garden

Esplanade

River Savoyard

Bastion

Burying Ground

Magazine

The site of Fort Ponchartrain is shown by the dotted enclosure, at A of all ranks.

★★★★★★

Resuming his march two hours before dawn, he came before day-break in sight of their position. Not a single outpost had been thrown out; the Americans were all asleep; and the British line was half formed within musket-shot of them before their sentries had remarked any-thing unusual. A rapid onset would have ended matters there and then with the bayonet. Instead of this Proctor halted, unlimbered his guns, and proceeded to wake up the whole of the enemy by a cannonade. There was in front of the village a stout palisade, behind which the American marksmen took shelter and opened a most destructive fire. In spite of all efforts no impression could be made upon the enemy at this point, though the American right, which was on the open ground, was swept away by the militia and Indians in utter rout.

After an hour's fighting Proctor, taking advantage of this success, turned the right of the palisade and drove the remnant of the enemy into some blockhouses, which they had constructed since their arrival. Here, however, they still maintained an obstinate defence until Gen-eral Winchester, who had been captured among the fugitives of the American right, sent them an order to surrender. Some six hundred prisoners were taken, and it was reckoned that fully three hundred men of the American force perished by bullet or tomahawk. In a word, the success was complete, and Winchester's column was almost annihilated. (Richardson, *War of 1812*).

But Proctor's losses were also very heavy, amounting to twenty-four white men killed and one hundred and fifty-eight, including of-ficers, wounded. The three companies of the Forty-First alone count-ed one hundred and twelve casualties, which cannot have been much less than half of their entire number.

It seems to be beyond question that most of these lives were un-necessarily sacrificed owing to the tactical blunders of Proctor. His instant resolution to take the offensive, the rapidity of his movements, and his final approach to the American position before dawn are de-serving of all praise; but his failure to turn his advantages to account, and his mishandling of the troops in action, stamp him for what he was, a bad commander.

However, the success at Frenchtown made a brilliant close to the campaign of 1812. The Americans had frittered away their strength at the straits of Detroit and Niagara, and had not only accomplished nothing, but had been well beaten and humiliated. On Lake Cham-

42

BATTLE OF FRENCHTOWN (OR RIVER RAISIN)

SKETCH MAP OF OPERATIONS OF THE
RIGHT DIVISION OF CANADIAN ARMY
AND THE
LEFT DIVISION OF AMERICAN ARMY
1812-'13
Scale of Miles

LAKE HURON

LAKE ONTARIO

UPPER CANADA

MICHIGAN

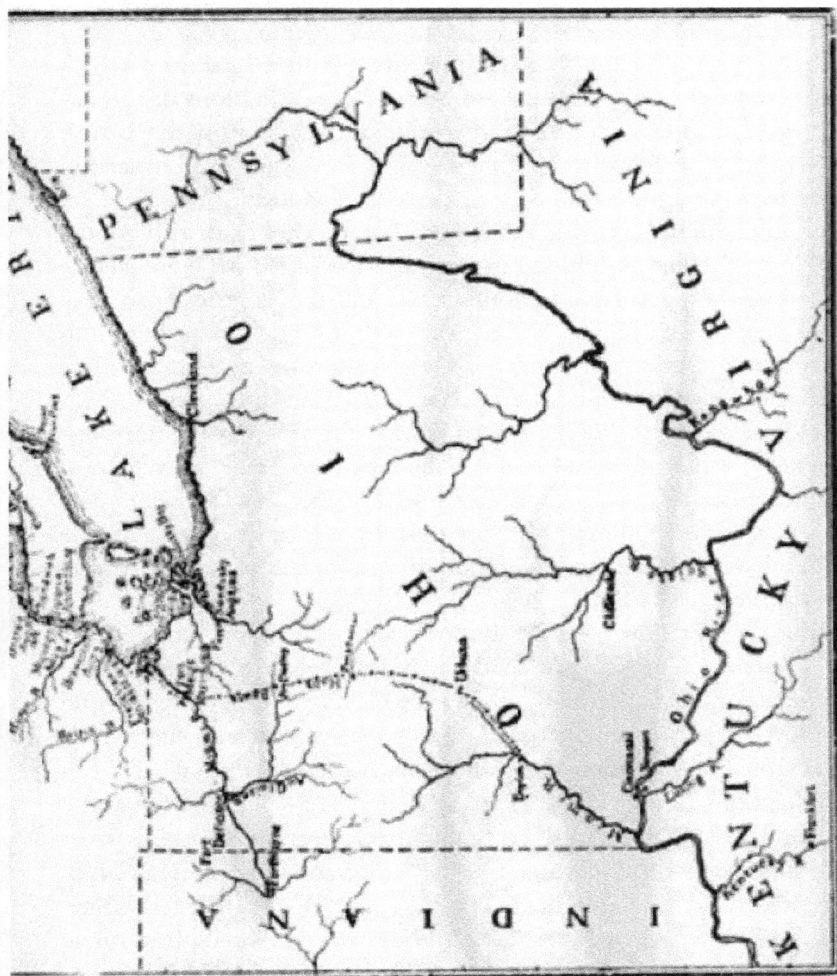

plain, where their real effort should have been made with all possible strength and resolution, they had failed even to attempt active operations. In plain words, their plan of campaign had been futile, and its execution feeble beyond contempt; and the result was increased embitterment of feeling between the two parties in America which had advocated or opposed the war. The internal divisions of the nation were further widened by the judicious conduct of the British Government, which at the outbreak of hostilities gave to all American shipping in British harbours free departure and safe protection on their voyage home, provided that they took cargoes of British goods.

Under the Act prohibiting the importation of British merchandise these cargoes were liable to confiscation; but the American Government had not strength to enforce this law; and after an acrimonious debate in Congress the whole of the forfeitures were remitted. The British Government also gave licences to all American vessels which would carry corn to the British Army in Spain; whereby the northern provinces, which detested the war and owned nearly the whole of the American shipping, reaped considerable profit at the expense of their southern neighbours. Prevost, in spite of all difficulties, was able to purchase and send to Wellington at a moderate price nearly four thousand barrels of flour.

But on the other hand the outlook for 1813 was far from cheerful. Captain Chauncey was working indefatigably to secure for the Americans naval superiority upon Lake Ontario, and before the end of November had launched a ship of six hundred tons within nine weeks of the day when the timber for her construction had been felled. So industrious and energetic a man was a dangerous foe at the best of times; the more so since, though the American Army—or what passed for such—had covered itself with disgrace, the American Navy had gained considerable credit. Four several British frigates, which had foolishly engaged American vessels of superior strength in single action, were shattered to pieces and taken with small loss to their adversaries, whose ships were not only well built and well manned, but bravely fought and skilfully manoeuvred. These victories were sufficient to hearten the Americans to further efforts, and to outweigh any effect that might have been produced by Prevost's fatal policy of conciliation.

Wellington, far away in Portugal and with imperfect information, passed his usual shrewd comment upon the event.

I have been very uneasy about the American naval successes. I think we should have peace with America before the season for opening the campaign in Canada if we could take one or two of their d—— d frigates.—*Wellington Desp.* To Beresford, 6th Feb. 1813.

LAKE ONTARIO

Dearborn (5,000)

Vincent (2,300)

FT. NIAGARA

YOUNGSTOWN

NEWARK

FT. GEORGE

QUEENSTON

LEWISTON

ST. DAVID'S

STAMFORD

BEECHWOODS

THOROLD

HAMILTON

Actually an amphibious operation along nearest lines. Preliminary bombardment and continued support by naval gunfire. First waves of light troops to clear beaches for main force, which followed. Reading reserve held out for support or exploitation. Jointly planned and secured by Scott and Perry.

Two troops of dragoons with mission to cut off British retreat to Queenstown. Delayed by artillery fire, they arrived too late.

From this position Brown reconnoitered as far as Ft. George.

Pursuit called off immediately after battle.

Pursuit started evening of 28 May; resumed next morning.

Pursuit begun in earnest 2 June

NOTE: Vincent reported that intensity of naval and arty. gunfire prevented effective opposition to the landing. This accounts for small American losses of 17 killed and 42 wounded.

CAPTURE OF FORT GEORGE
27 May 1813

BROWN'S CAMPAIGN
3 July — 21 September 1814

THE WAR OF 1812

Operations Along the Niagara River,
May 1813–September 1814

SCALE OF MILES

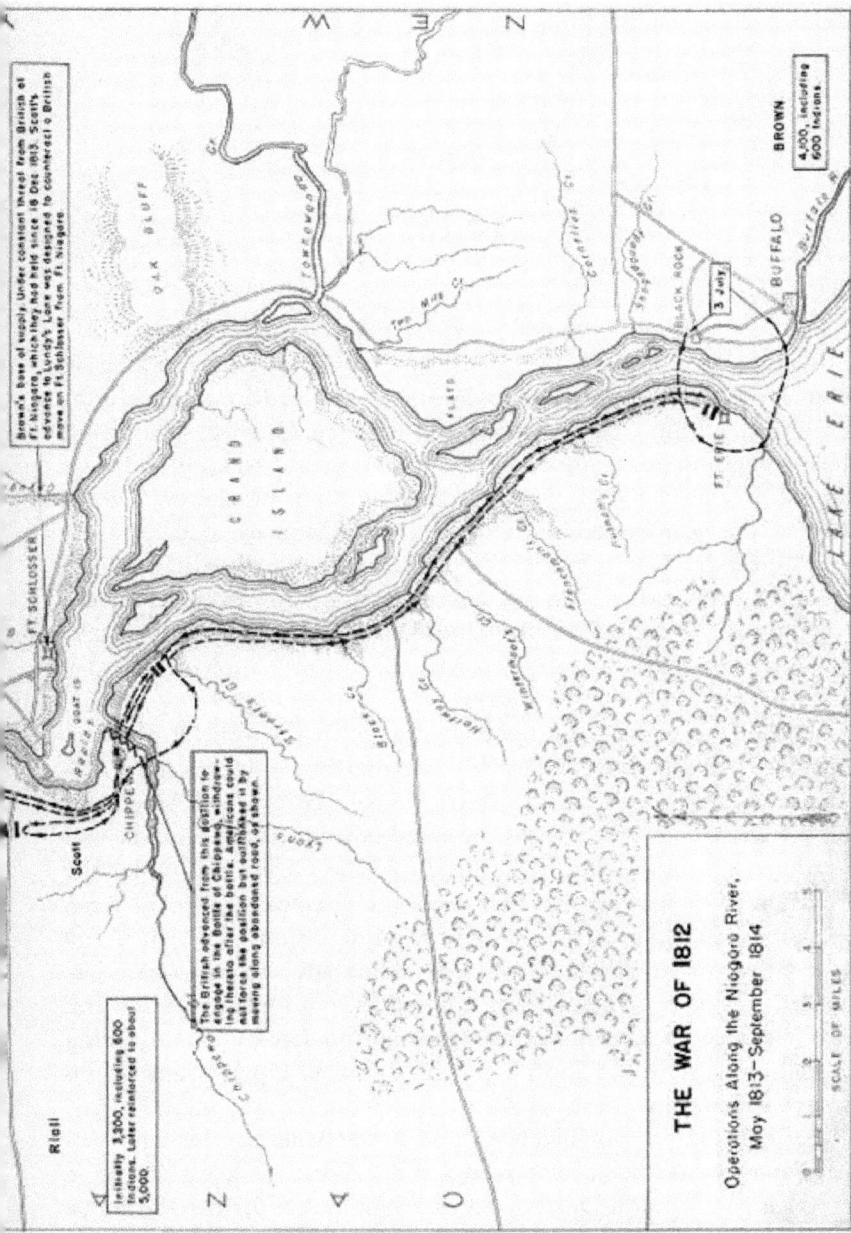

Brown's Base of supply. Under constant threat from British at Ft Niagara, which they had held since 19 Dec 1813. Scott's advance to Lundy's Lane was designed to counteract a British move on Ft Schlosser from Ft Niagara.

BROWN

4,100, including 600 Indians.

3 July

FT ERIE

BLACK ROCK

BUFFALO

LAKE ERIE

FT SCHLOSSER

GRAND ISLAND

OAK BLUFF

Scott

CHIPPEWA

The British advanced from this position to engage in the Battle of Chippewa, withdrawing thereto after the battle. Americans could not force the position but outflanked it by moving along abandoned road, of shown.

Riall

Initially 3,000, including 600 Indians. Later reinforced to about 5,000.

CHAPTER 2
1813

At the close of 1812, the Americans, instead of concentrating all their efforts upon the capture of Kingston and of Montreal, so as to sever Upper from Lower Canada and threaten Quebec, squandered their strength in petty operations about Detroit and Niagara, and were handsomely beaten at all points; redeeming their mistake only at the close of the year by sending Commodore Chauncey to build a superior fleet on Lake Ontario. Nevertheless the party that favoured war, though mortified, was not discouraged. Madison was re-elected President at the end of the year; and the sanguine found consolation in the retreat of Wellington from Madrid and in Napoleon's victory at Borodino.

The spring of 1813 brought no change in the general position. General Harrison remained with one American force on the Maumee, faced by Proctor on the Detroit River; British and Americans still glared at each other across the rapid current of the Niagara; and Dearborn still reposed near the head of Lake Champlain under the eye of Prevost's detachments. Moreover, the directors of the American operations seemed to have learned little wisdom from experience; and even Commodore Chauncey himself, while advocating an early attack on and capture of Kingston, could foresee no further result from that operation than American ascendancy on Lake Ontario, failing to realise that it would also necessarily throw all Upper Canada into American hands.

Early in the year intelligence came to the American headquarters that Kingston had been reinforced and that Prevost had arrived there in person; whereupon Dearborn took fright lest the British should be meditating an attack upon Sackett's Harbour. As a matter of fact Prevost did pay a flying visit to the posts in Upper Canada in February, and had ordered, as shall presently be seen, reinforcements to Kingston; but Dearborn's apprehensive eye saw danger where as yet there was none, and inspired his superiors at Washington with his own alarms. The orders given to him, therefore, were to assemble four thousand men at Sackett's Harbour and three thousand at Buffalo; the former force to attack in succession Kingston and York, with the help of Chauncey's fleet, and then in combination with the troops at Buffalo to assail the British frontier at Niagara—or in other words, as it has been aptly expressed, to begin to fell the tree by lopping off its branches.

On the British side the Admiralty, warned by the disasters which had befallen English frigates, and encouraged by the failure of France in Russia, increased the naval force on the American coast, especially in the matter of ships of the line, and in the course of the spring established an effective blockade from the mouth of the Mississippi almost to Rhode Island. The outlets of the Chesapeake and Delaware above all were strictly watched, the war having been brought on by the middle and southern states; while the ports of New England, where the conflict was unpopular, were for the most part left open.

This was the measure which in due time reduced America to exhaustion; but the process, being gradual, could not produce its effect at once. For more immediate service the Secretary of State had promised in December to send three battalions at once to Bermuda, (13th; 2/41st; 98th), to proceed from thence to the St. Lawrence as soon as the river should be open; and Prevost was thus enabled to send a substantial reinforcement to Sheaffe at Kingston for the strengthening of the posts at Niagara and Detroit. (Half co. of Artillery; 18th; 6 cos. 104th; 4 cos. Canadian Voltigeurs, the 104th had arrived in New Brunswick late in 1812; and this detachment had marched overland to Quebec).

All, however, turned upon the naval command of the Lakes, and here the situation was less promising. On Lake Ontario the British had two ships at York, and two more, besides two on the stocks, at Kingston; whereas the Americans had eight vessels in all, many of them trifling in size, but the two largest of them superior to the two largest of the British. On Lake Erie the British had three vessels afloat and three more building; the Americans had but one afloat, but on the other hand they had Lieutenant Perry, an officer of admirable skill and energy, in command at Erie, who was labouring with his whole soul to increase his squadron.

The Americans too, having far larger resources both in material

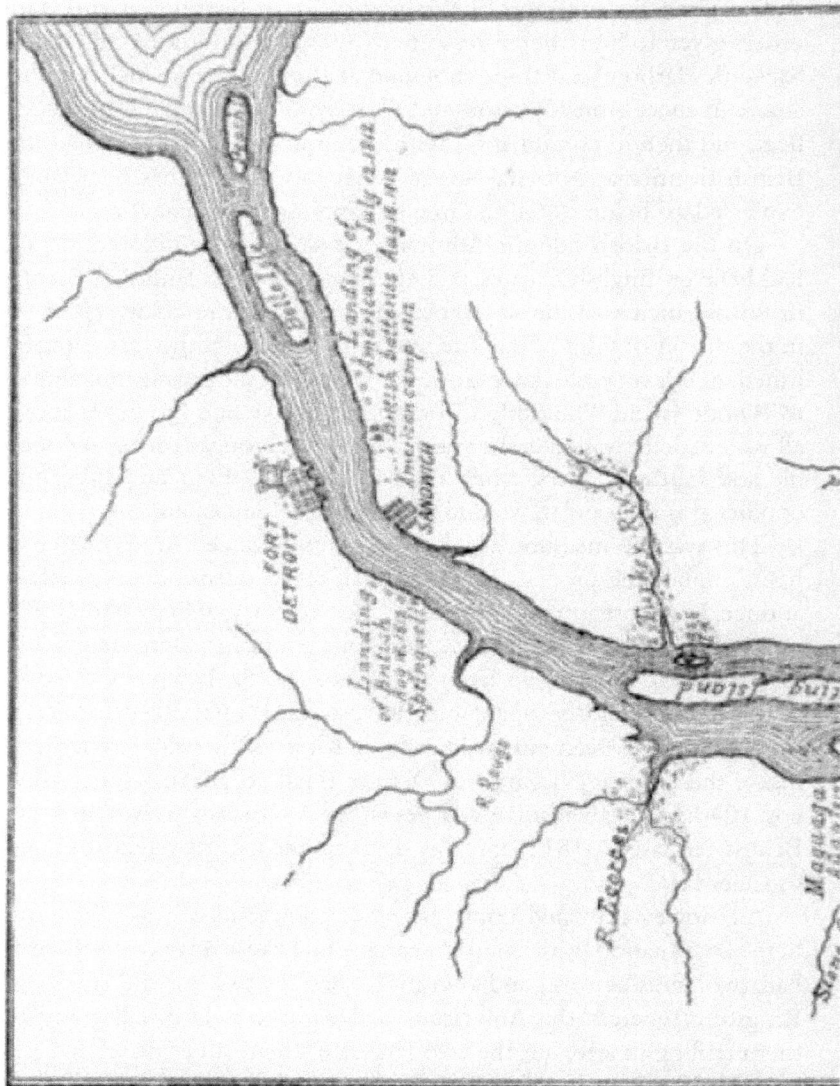

Bois Blc

Landing of Americans July 12 1812

British batteries Magazine

American camp etc

SANDWICH

FORT DETROIT

Landing of British troops which Springwell

R. Rouge

Turkey River

Grosse Island

R. Escorces

Maguaga Indians

Stone

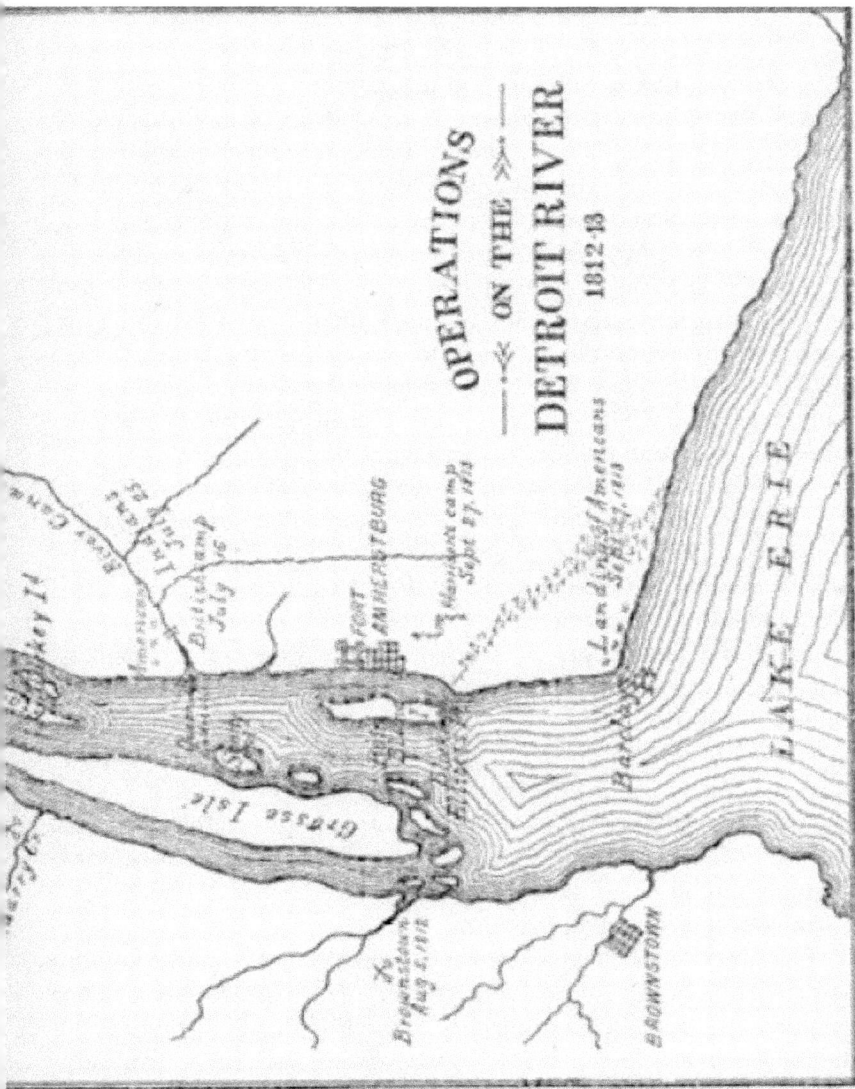

OPERATIONS
——— ON THE ———
DETROIT RIVER
1812-13

LAKE ERIE

Grosse Isle

FORT
AMHERSTBURG

Harrison camp
Sept 27, 1813

Landing of Americans
Sept 27, 1813

Bois Blanc

Battle

BROWNSTOWN

To
Brownstown
Aug 5, 1812

British camp
July 16

River Canard

Turkey Id

and population close at hand, enjoyed an immense advantage over the British in the matter of shipbuilding. Lastly, the British were much embarrassed by dearth of seamen and of officers. In March one of Prevost's staff reported that on Lake Ontario there was not a man fit to command a man-of-war, and that additional officers also were needed. The Admiralty had promised to send out a naval captain to take charge of the naval force, besides a certain number of sailors and artificers; but even so the Americans, particularly after the blockade became effectual and great part of their merchant shipping was laid up, could always supply far better crews than their adversaries. (Prevost to Sec. of State 17th, 19th March, 2nd April 1813; with enclosures).

The campaign opened with an attack upon one of the foremost American posts upon the St. Lawrence at Ogdensburg, from whence the enemy had made repeated nocturnal depredations upon the surrounding country. The enterprise on its small scale was completely successful, and resulted after a sharp fight in the capture of seventy-four prisoners, and the taking or destruction of eleven guns, four armed vessels and a quantity of arms and stores. (The troops engaged were detachments of the R.A., 8th, Glengarry Fencibles, Newfoundland Regiment, and Militia; and their losses were 8 men killed, 8 officers and 44 men wounded).

This, however, was but an isolated affair; and the serious business of the campaign began in April with the first of the operations prescribed to Dearborn. By the 19th of that month Sackett's Harbour was clear of ice; and on the 27th, after being driven back once by heavy weather, Chauncey's squadron with eighteen hundred troops on board appeared before York. Sheaffe was here in command of four companies of regular and fencible troops, besides militia and dockyard workmen, in all about six hundred men; and he had several hours' warning of the enemy's approach.

The Americans landed to the west of the town; and Sheaffe, having no defences except a ruined fort and five guns (of which three had no trunnions), detached two companies of the Eighth and a company of the Newfoundland regiment—together about two hundred and fifty strong—about two hundred militia and a handful of Indians to hold the enemy in check, while he destroyed the public stores and prepared for a retreat.

It should seem that Captain McNeill of the Eighth, upon ascertaining the point of landing, drew up his men in full view of the American ships and at half range of cannon-shot, with the natural result that an American broadside mowed down half of his men and killed the captain himself. The remainder retired into a wood behind the shore, and with their comrades resisted for a long time most desperately and gallantly, until driven back by superior numbers upon the fort. The Americans swarmed after them but were checked by the blowing up of the magazine, which made havoc both among assailants and defenders.

Under cover of this explosion, accidental or intentional, Sheaffe brought off most of the survivors of his force after an action of eight hours. Of his regular troops sixty-two were killed, thirty-four wounded and saved, forty-two wounded and prisoners, seventeen missing or captured unhurt. The Eighth, out of just under two hundred men, lost forty-five killed and forty-nine wounded, and the Newfoundland regiment, out of one weak company, twelve killed and twenty wounded, but only four unwounded prisoners.

The militia, who were left to surrender the town, laid down their arms without disgrace, to the number of two hundred and sixty. Altogether it was not a discreditable little fight, though beyond doubt McNeill sacrificed many lives by his wanton and foolish defiance of the enemy's guns. The American loss exceeded three hundred, their commander, General Pike, being among those who perished through the explosion.

Upon entering into possession of York, which, though little more than a village, was the capital of the province, the American troops took leave of all control. Contrary to the articles of capitulation, the public buildings and all the records were burned, the church was robbed, the public library pillaged to the last book, and much private property plundered and destroyed. Too much must not be made of excesses to which all troops have at times given way; but it is less pleasant to learn that the American rank and file subjected the unfortunate inhabitants in cold blood to every kind of insult as well as to depredation. (Major Allan of the Militia to Sheaffe. 2nd May 1813).

Insolent crowing is the one thing which the weaker party can never forgive in an enemy; and the nation which indulges in it must look for bitter reprisals.

One ship only, a small schooner, was taken at York, and another on the stocks was destroyed, yet Chauncey flattered himself that he had dealt the British a blow from which they could not recover, and that his next stroke would accomplish the conquest of Upper Canada. Accordingly, after three days spent in the destruction or loading of the

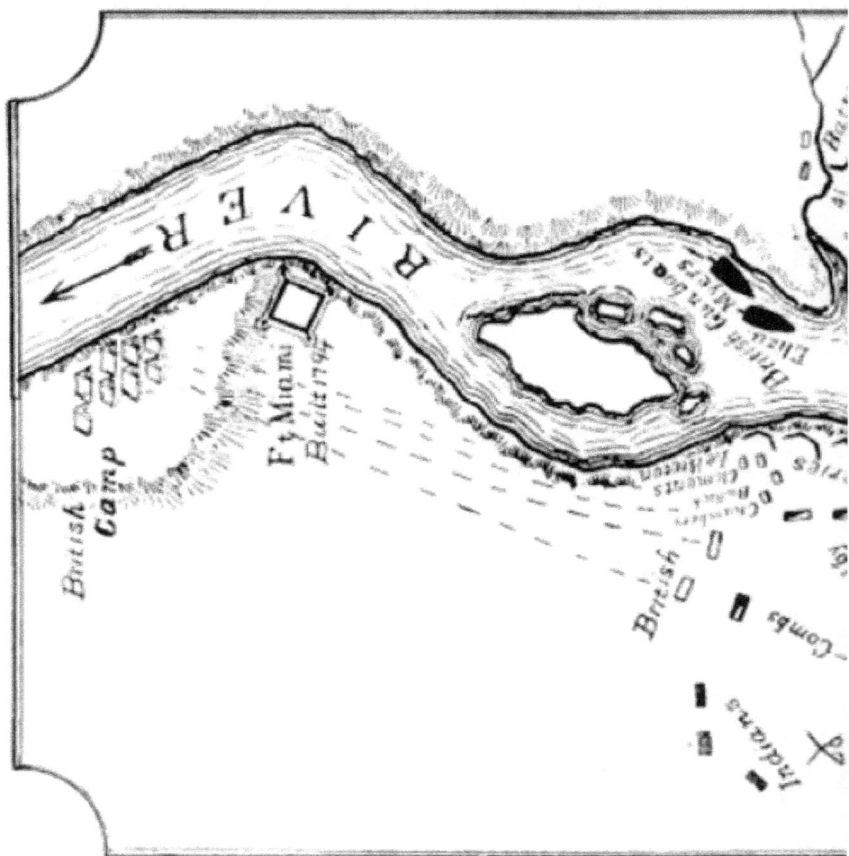

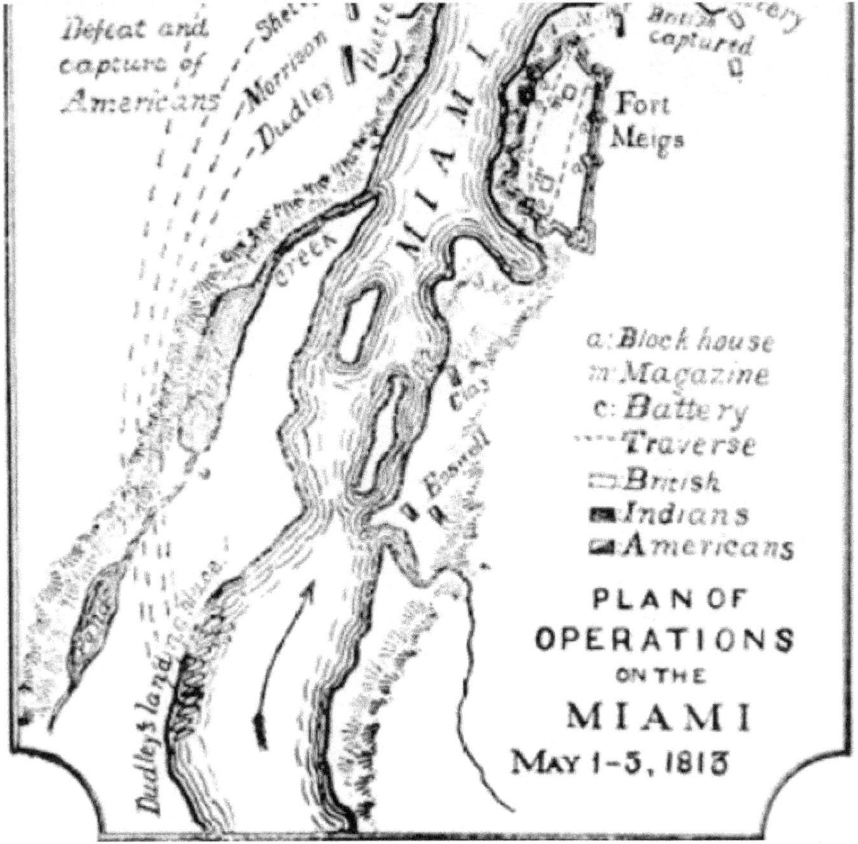

PLAN OF
OPERATIONS
ON THE
MIAMI
May 1–5, 1813

a: Blockhouse
m. Magazine
c: Battery
---- Traverse
⬜ Brush
⬛ Indians
▨ Americans

Fort
Meigs

British Battery
captured

MIAMI

Harrison

Dudley I.

Defeat and
capture of
Americans

Dudley's landing place

captured stores, the American armament evacuated York on the 1st of May with intent to sail to Fort Niagara, but owing to foul winds did not reach it until the 8th.

Then, on account of the sickliness of the troops, who were much crowded in the ships, it was decided to defer the attack and return to Sackett's Harbour. A few days later Chauncey sent a flag of truce into Kingston, and, after hearing the report of the officer who carried it, decided to remain himself for the present at Sackett's Harbour, ask for reinforcements, and take charge of its defence. He was not wrong, for Prevost had again arrived there, bringing with him Captain Sir James Yeo, a brilliant young officer of the navy, who had reached Quebec from England on the 5th with a small body of British sailors.

Four ships of strength were awaiting his orders—two of the original squadron, one which had fortunately sailed over from York just before the American attack, and a fourth newly built but ready for service; besides which a fifth was on the stocks. Moreover, reckoning on fresh reinforcements from Europe, Prevost had ordered a thousand to eleven hundred troops to Upper Canada, (1 troop of Canadian dragoons; half co. R.A.; 1/1st; 4 cos. Grenadiers); so that there was a formidable force both afloat and ashore to contest the mastery of the Lake with the Americans. (Mahan, *War of 1812*, ii. Prevost to Sec. of State, 18th May 1813, 2 letters).

However, reinforcements having meanwhile arrived at Sackett's Harbour, the first division of the American armament sailed again for Niagara on the 20th, and disembarked its troops next day in rear of that fort. On the 25th Chauncey arrived with a second division, making up a total of six to seven thousand troops; and after a day spent in reconnaissance, Dearborn decided to attack at dawn of the 27th.

The British force at Fort George numbered about eleven hundred regular troops of all ranks, (R.A., with some men of the 41st for gunners; 5 cos. 8th; detachments Glengarry and Newfoundland regiments), and three hundred militia, under command of Brigadier-general Vincent. The fort itself carried four heavy cannon, which had been captured at Detroit; and a fifth had been mounted *en barbette* about half a mile below it. The British force was therefore considerably overmatched, but Vincent none the less determined to resist to the utmost.

At daybreak a number of flat-bottomed boats, covered by the guns of the American ships of war, were seen making for the shore of the lake almost half a mile west of the mouth of the river; and at the same

time Fort Niagara opened fire upon Fort George. The cannonade was interrupted for a time by a heavy fog, but, when that lifted, three schooners took up a position in the river and, in conjunction with the ships on the lake, swept the low ground about Fort George with a cross-fire. The single gun mounted towards the lake was soon silenced, and the village of Newark, being interposed between Fort George and the lake, prevented the cannon of the fort from being brought to bear in this direction.

Vincent drew out every man that he could spare, leaving only fifty regulars and eighty militia to defend the fort, and divided his force into three small columns, with the Glengarry and Newfoundland men, aided by a few Indians, in advance. These brave fellows, after trying in vain to resist the landing, were driven back by the storm of cannon-shot upon their supports; but rallying on these—about three hundred and twenty of the Eighth and half as many militia—they faced about in a patch of brushwood, and, always under the cross-fire of artillery, strove desperately to stem the enemy's advance.

The effort was hopeless; and, after suffering very heavy loss, Vincent retreated in perfect order southward to St. David's and thence westward to Beaver Dam. Before doing so he sent orders to draw off the troops from Fort George; but through some miscarriage or mistake they were left behind, and so fell into the enemy's hands, being the only unwounded prisoners taken by them that day.

The garrisons of Chippewa and Fort Erie, being summoned in time, joined the main body safely at Beaver Dam that night; and on the following day Vincent continued his retreat unmolested to Forty Mile Creek (the modern Grimsby), finally halting on the 29th at Burlington Heights (the modern Hamilton), where he turned with some sixteen hundred men and stood at bay.

This was a spirited little fight, most creditable to the troops but not so to their commander. The detachments of the Eighth, Glengarry, Newfoundland and Militia, together under six hundred strong, lost no fewer than three hundred and ninety of all ranks killed and wounded, the Eighth alone having two hundred and two casualties. Yet this slaughter was absolutely purposeless. Vincent must have known that no possible object could be gained by pushing his men into a fight against four times their numbers under a cross-fire of artillery; and Fort George might just as well have been abandoned at the cost of twenty men as of four hundred, particularly as the number of British soldiers in the whole country was very small. But, whether owing to the insolence of American speakers in Congress, or to contempt for the American troops—still very raw—in the field, British officers appear to have made it a point of honour never to retire without resisting to the utmost, or in other words without sacrificing valuable troops for a purely sentimental object.

However, on the 2nd of June Vincent reported his men to be in great spirits, and anxious for an order to return to Fort George; and, though the enemy had pushed an advanced guard of four hundred horse and foot to Fifteen Mile Creek, with two thousand more at Twelve Mile Creek, he felt confident that they would not dare to attack him. (Vincent to Prevost, 2nd June; in Prevost to Sec. of State, 6th June 1813).

Meanwhile, upon the night after the American landing at Fort George, Prevost, with the object of making a diversion, embarked between seven and eight hundred men (1st Royal Scots; 2 cos. 8th; 4 cos. 104th; 2 cos. Canadian Voltigeurs; 1 co. Glengarry L.I.; R.A. with 2 guns),1 from Kingston upon five men-of-war, and sailed for Sackett's Harbour.

★★★★★★

There is some confusion as to the date. Prevost in his letter to Bathurst of 1st June says that he arrived off Sackett's Harbour at daybreak of the 27th, and this date, though quite irreconcilable with the rest of the letter, has been accepted by Capt. Mahan and Kingsford. Nevertheless 27th is obviously a slip of the pen for 28th, for Prevost says that he did not order the troops to embark until he had heard that Fort George had been cannonaded for 24 hours, and the cannonade of Fort George began at 4 a.m. of the 27th. It is very plain, therefore, that the expedition did not sail until the late hours of the 27th or the earliest of the 28th. The *Life of Sir G. Prevost* says that it sailed in the night of the 27th, which is doubtless correct.

★★★★★★

The time was not unpropitious, for at the moment there were only two men-of-war and four hundred troops in the place. (So say Capt. Mahan and *History of the War*, a very partial narrative; but the American General Wilkinson—quoted by Kingsford, viii.—states the number of regulars at 787).

Light and baffling winds, however, prevented the armament from drawing close to the harbour until evening of the 28th, and in the meantime the American commander, Colonel Jacob Brown, had time to summon to him five hundred militia. Sackett's Harbour itself lies on the south side of a bay named Black River Bay, which runs from south-west to north-east out of Lake Ontario; the haven being formed by a narrow peninsula which juts out for some distance in a north-westerly direction, and then throws a long narrow spit to the eastward. Within the space thus enclosed is the anchorage; and upon the spit, called Navy Point, was the naval establishment.

On the shore over against Navy Point were situated in succession from north-east to south-west a work called Fort Volunteer, a battery of three guns and a blockhouse; and at the north-eastern angle of the peninsula stood another work, enclosing a blockhouse, named Fort Tompkins. At the north-western corner of the peninsula lies Horse Island, connected with the mainland by a fordable causeway or neck, which offered a convenient point for disembarkation, and had been in fact chosen by Colonel Baynes, who was in command of the landing party, for that purpose.

Accordingly at ten o'clock on the night of the 28th the boats were assembled round the fleet, and soon afterwards they pulled off, with a gunboat in advance. Brown, fully prepared for the attack and divining its probable direction, drew up his militia in first line at the end of the neck, holding his regular troops in reserve in second line. Baynes meanwhile led his boats forward in the order which the troops were to assume when landed, and successfully threw his men ashore upon Horse Island. This done he launched the grenadier-company of the Hundredth against the militia, which with one field-gun occupied the farther end of the causeway.

Though the passage was but four feet broad, in many places under water, and two hundred yards long, the grenadiers fell upon the militia before they could fire more than one volley from their muskets or one round from their gun, captured the field-piece and scattered the militiamen in all directions. The rest of the force then came up, and separating into two columns pressed on into the woods, which were alive with the fire of the American regulars. The British gunboats poured their shot blindly into the trees; but the Americans resisted stoutly and were only dislodged by the bayonet, when they fled in disorder to their blockhouse. In the confusion an American officer, thinking that all was lost, set fire to the navy-yard, and to the outward eye the success of the British seemed to be complete. As a matter of fact they had come to the end of their resources. They needed heavier ordnance than fieldpieces or the light carronades in the gunboats to produce any impression upon the blockhouse and forts; and failure of wind prevented the men-of-war from taking any part in the action.

Prevost therefore called his men off and abandoned the enterprise, enabling the Americans to extinguish the flames in the navy-yard before any great damage had been done. His losses amounted to forty-eight of all ranks killed and two hundred and twenty-one wounded, of which latter a few fell into the enemy's hands. The casualties of the enemy were probably rather more numerous, for Prevost brought away with him one hundred and fifty prisoners, besides three guns.

Frantic vituperation was heaped upon Prevost for his conduct upon this day; and it is still represented that he stopped his troops while they were rushing in upon the flood-tide of victory. It must, however, be admitted that his position was extremely difficult. More than one-third of his men had fallen; and, though the bulk of his enemy appears to have been completely beaten, it is more than doubtful whether, without heavy artillery, scaling ladders or appliances of any kind, he could have stormed the strongly stockaded works, possession of which would alone have made him master of Sackett's Harbour.

★★★★★★

Mr. Kingsford says:

Surely heavy guns could have been brought up from the ships and the place battered down.

But ships' guns, unless mounted on travelling carriages, are not so easily moved.

★★★★★★

It must be remembered too that the naval yard was seen to be in flames, and that the destruction of the stores and the ships on the stocks was, after all, the principal object of the attack. Further, it must be admitted that luck was against him, light winds having in the first place given the enemy twenty-four hours in which to gather reinforcements, and, in the second, prevented the heavy guns of the ships from coming into action. The American commander, Brown, a brave and capable officer, declared that unless Prevost had retreated when he did, not a man of his force would have returned to Kingston; and on the whole it seems to me that the British commander had no alternative other than retreat.

Yet the enterprise was worth attempting; and it appears to me unjust to characterise it, in the words of a judicial American historian, (Capt. Mahan), as irresolute. Doubtless Prevost would have done better to employ a larger force; but this was impossible for him except at the cost of long delay; and the essence of the whole operation was to fall swiftly upon the American naval base, while the bulk of the American troops were employed at Niagara.

But an attack which costs the assailants more than a third of their numbers, and is only abandoned because an essential part of the plan—naval co-operation—fails unavoidably through no fault of the commander, can hardly be called irresolute. The conduct of the British was superb, as their losses sufficiently show; (see list below), but credit is due also to the American regular troops, who must have turned their advantages in forest-fighting to good account and maintained the struggle stubbornly and well.

E.g.:

8th (2 cos.)	5 killed,		6 officers,		70 men wounded.
100th (1 co.)	6 „		0 „		23 „
104th (4 cos.)	22 „		7 „		62 „
Glengarry L.I. (1 co.)	6 „		2 „		18 „

The result of the operations so far was that, on the one side, the capture of Fort George had prevented the British ship *Queen Charlotte* from taking supplies from that depot to Amherstburg; and that, on the other, the fitting out of the new American ship at Sackett's Harbour had been delayed for three weeks. But more than this, Chauncey was considerably discouraged. He had altogether fourteen vessels, mounting sixty-two guns; while Yeo had thirteen, including six gunboats, mounting one hundred and six guns; yet although the ordnance on the gunboats was paltry, he allowed Yeo to sail unmolested on the 3rd of June with stores, supplies and reinforcements for Vincent. (Flank companies of 104th, and a detachment of the Glengarry L.I.).

Meanwhile Vincent had taken his own measures for ridding himself of his enemy. His position at Burlington Heights, though strong, was too much extended for a force which, after calling in a small detachment from Fort Erie, did not exceed eighteen hundred of all ranks; and his information indicated that the Americans were closing in upon him not only in his front, but on his right flank by land and on his left by water. His position was the more critical inasmuch as he was short both of supplies and of ammunition, and in the event of mishap had no line of retreat except to York, while his abandonment of Burlington Heights would yield to the enemy the British line of communication by land with Detroit.

The central column of the enemy, consisting of two brigades of infantry, a detachment of dragoons and eight or nine guns, in all between three and four thousand men, reached Stony Creek, about seven miles from his camp, on the 5th of June. There it was reconnoitred by Colonel Harvey of Vincent's staff, who upon his return recommended a night attack. Accordingly at half-past eleven detachments of the Eighth and Forty-Ninth, together nearly eight hundred of all ranks, marched off into the darkness, and by two o'clock in the morning of the 6th the whole had arrived unperceived within three hundred yards of the enemy's camp.

The outlying sentries were bayoneted " in the quietest manner," to use Harvey's own words; but, in spite of strict orders to the contrary, the men began shouting and firing before they were deployed for the attack, and the enemy, springing to their arms, opened fire. Thereupon Major Plenderleath of the Forty-Ninth appears to have dashed forward at once against the American guns; and a confused combat ensued in the darkness, both sides firing indiscriminately upon friends and foes, with the result that after about an hour's affray the Americans withdrew, leaving Generals Winder and Chandler, and over one hundred and twenty more officers and men, together with four pieces of cannon, in the hands of the British.

Harvey, who was in charge of the attack, called off his troops before daylight should reveal the paucity of their numbers; but some fifty soldiers, either not hearing or disobeying the order to retire, fell into the enemy's hands. The cost to Vincent of the whole operation was just over two hundred of all ranks killed, wounded and missing. (Killed, 1 officer, 22 men; wounded, 12 officers, 124 men; missing, 55 men. Total, 214).

The affair was less successful and more costly than it should have been, but, thanks to the good luck which had thrown the American commander and his second into Vincent's hands, it was sufficient. Their successor at once retreated to Forty Mile Creek, embarking his wounded on the flotilla of boats which carried his supplies and baggage on the lake. On the 8th of June, however, Yeo's squadron came upon the scene, and his gunboats began to bombard the enemy's camp, while two companies of the Eighth were disembarked to assail it by land. Thereupon the Americans again retreated, leaving a quantity of stores behind them, burned Fort Erie on the 9th, and, withdrawing all detachments in the strait, concentrated their force about Fort George.

Yeo cruised along the south coast of Lake Ontario, capturing vessels and destroying or appropriating quantities of stores. Vincent, having received his reinforcements from the Commodore, prepared to take the offensive, pushing his advanced parties forward to about Twenty Mile Creek, Ten Mile Creek, and Beaver Dam, the latter post being under command of Lieutenant Fitzgibbon of the Forty-Ninth. On the 23rd of June an American detachment of nearly six hundred men under Colonel Boerstler was pushed forward against the place last named, but was ambushed by Indians early on the morning of the 24th, and after three hours' confused fighting was awed into surrender by a judicious movement of Fitzgibbon's detachment across its line of retreat. From that moment the American Army of Niagara was paralysed, the War Department having given orders that nothing more was to be attempted until naval superiority should have been established on Lake Ontario. So fruitful had been Vincent's bold assumption of the offensive by Harvey's advice at Stony Creek.

Naval superiority, however, was very shortly about to assert itself, for on the 12th of June the vessel which had been saved from the flames a fortnight earlier, was launched by the Americans at Sackett's Harbour and named the *General Pike*. Armed, as she was to be, with twenty-six long twenty-four-pounders, she would be a match in certain circumstances for the entire British squadron combined, every ship of which mounted only the short cannon known as carronades, which had not half the range of the long guns.

Yeo accordingly conceived a second plan for surprising a part of Chauncey's squadron by land with about seven hundred men, one-third of them soldiers of the Royal Scots and Hundredth Foot, and the remainder blue-jackets. He had advanced to within ten miles of Sackett's Harbour unperceived, and had lain hidden for twenty-four hours in the forest intending to make a night attack, when by the information of two deserters of the Newfoundland regiment the enemy was set on the alert, and the project was perforce abandoned. This happened at the very end of June; and Prevost, who conceived the British to be already inferior on the water, decided that he too would abstain from any offensive movement about Niagara until British naval ascendancy should be assured.

Thus both sides practically abjured all enterprise in the field, and concentrated all their efforts on their dockyards. Though the true issue of the entire campaign undoubtedly turned upon the naval operations, it may be questioned whether either side were right in pursuing this policy. It was demoralising for the Americans to sit still about Fort

SKETCH
OF THE
STONEY CREEK BATTLE GROUND
June 1813.

George, while an enemy of much inferior force lay unentrenched within five miles of them; but it would have been far more demoralising if Prevost had taken advantage of their late discomfiture to keep them in constant alarm.

The occupation of Fort George was in itself a serious inconvenience, since it interrupted the British communications by land with Lake Erie; and the arrival of the Thirteenth Foot, seven hundred strong, at Quebec from the West Indies at the end of June might well have heartened Prevost to an energetic offensive. There was, as he confessed, little fear of an attack by Lake Champlain, and the less since some of the enemy's armed vessels had been recently on the St. Lawrence.

Of course the expulsion of the Americans from Niagara would not hurt Chauncey, yet it was likely to weaken his nerve, which was already shaken by the mishaps which had lately befallen the American Army, and to set the military commander quarrelling with him. But there are very few men who are qualified to direct the joint operations of a squadron and an army, and unfortunately Prevost was not one of them. Supremacy on Lake Ontario was the navy's business; let the navy look to it first, and the military operations would follow afterwards; if the navy were slow, let it be hurried. Such were the principles which he cherished only too faithfully to the end of the war.

His conduct was the more blameworthy inasmuch as the Admiralty, by sending ships enough to blockade the American ports and harry their coasting trade, was rapidly bringing home to the United States the true meaning of war. To emphasise the lesson the British Government had despatched a special squadron under Sir John Warren, together with a small body of troops under Sir Sidney Beckwith, with orders to harry the American coast at large by constant descents. This armament sailed by way of Bermuda, where Beckwith exchanged a detachment of inferior troops against an equal number of men admirably trained by Colonel Charles Napier, and shortly afterwards sailed for the American shore with twenty-three hundred men organised into two brigades. (See list following).

★★★★★★

The force with which Beckwith sailed from England was 2434 marines, a detachment of 300 of the 103rd (mostly bad characters), and 2 independent companies of French deserters. At Bermuda he organised the force as follows:

Charles Napier's Brigade : R.M.A.	5 officers,	76	n.c.o. and men.	
2nd Batt. Marines . .	30	,,	72	,,
102nd	13	,,	310	,,
1st Independent Company .	5	,,	149	,,
Lieut-Col. Williams's Brigade : R.M.A.	5	,,	72	,,
Rocket Battery R.A. . .	2	,,	49	,,
1st Batt. Marines . . .	31	,,	730	,,
2nd Independent Company .	5	,,	148	,,
Total . . .	96	,,	2235	,,

★★★★★★

The operations of this force were so trifling that they may as well be dismissed at once. They consisted of no more than a raid upon Hampton Roads and the destruction of a small American detachment at Hampton itself, and of two abortive raids in other quarters, June 26, ending in the removal of the whole force to Nova Scotia in September. There were three commanders, Admiral Cockburn, Admiral Warren and General Beckwith; of whom Cockburn, an excellent sailor, tried to be a general, and Beckwith, an admirable soldier, attempted to play the admiral.

The most noteworthy feature of the operations, was that fifty men or the foreign independent companies committed to Beckwith's command deserted as soon as they were ashore, and the rest committed shameful atrocities. Many officers, indeed, in both services had relations in America, and hated the duty of destroying property which might belong to them.(Beckwith to Sec. of State, June 3rd, 28th, 1813; see also Napier's *Life of Sir Charles Napier*, i.).

Nevertheless the diversion was a useful one, and Prevost should have shown greater vigour in taking advantage of it. Every military success was bound to react not only upon the American Government and the American Army, but upon the American Navy also, making the sailors ask themselves for what object they risked their lives on the water if the soldiers were always beaten on land. On the contrary, Prevost was disposed rather to promote the like divisions in his own force, by keeping the troops inactive until the squadron should have prepared the way for them.

On the 20th of July the *General Pike* was ready for service, and on the following day Chauncey sailed out of Sackett's Harbour, arriving off Niagara on the 27th. After a fruitless attempt, in conjunction with the army, against the rear of Vincent's position at Burlington Heights, he returned to Niagara, where at daybreak of the 7th of August Yeo appeared with his whole force, namely, the *Wolfe* and Royal *George*, ships; *Melville* and *Moira*, brigs; *Sir Sidney Smith* and *Beresford*, schooners; the largest mounting twenty-three and the smallest twelve guns. Chauncey on his side had the *General Pike* of twenty-six guns, the *Madison* of twenty-four, the *Oneida* of eighteen, and sixteen small schooners, the largest of which carried ten guns and the smallest one or two.

The great bulk of the British cannon were of short range; the great bulk of the American of long range; and, since each commander was anxious above all things not to allow his rival to gain supremacy, neither was willing to engage except under the conditions that favoured himself. Accordingly the fleets manoeuvred for four days without further result than the capsizing of two of the American schooners in a squall; but on the night of the 10th they at last came into action, and Yeo succeeded in capturing two more of the schooners. On the 13th Chauncey returned to Sackett's Harbour to revictual, and owing to heavy weather and other causes it was nearly a month before the two fleets met again, (Sept. 7th), only to part once more after four or five days of manoeuvring without any approach to a decisive result.

Prevost's irritation was extreme. Ignoring the fact that the American ordnance gave Chauncey an advantage practically equivalent to that of a man who fights with a rifle against an enemy armed with a weapon of smooth bore, he expected Yeo to make short work of his adversary, so as not only to permit the army to resume operations, but to strengthen the fleet on Lake Erie with some of his seamen. Yet the commodore had really no alternative, he wrote to the Admiralty:

> I assure you, Sir, that the great advantage the enemy have over me from their big twenty-four-pounders almost precludes the possibility of success unless we can force them to close action, which they ever have avoided with the most studious circumspection.—Prevost to Sec. of State, 22nd Sept. 1813. The quotation from Yeo's report is given by Captain Mahan (ii.).

It would have been more profitable if Prevost, instead of blaming the navy for its inability to achieve the impossible, had done his best to reopen the communication with Lake Erie which the Americans had closed by the capture of Fort George.

The consequences of the long inaction on Lake Ontario soon showed itself. Ever since March Lieutenant Oliver Perry had been working with admirable energy at Fort Erie, not only to build and fit out a squadron which should ensure the command of the lake, but to procure a garrison and throw up works which should protect the vessels while still under construction. He met with no great support, for he could obtain only four small guns and five hundred militia; and it might have occurred to General Proctor that it would be well to spoil such a nest of possible mischief before the brood should be hatched. Proctor, however, was flying, as he thought, at higher game.

After the defeat of General Winchester in January General Harrison had reorganised his army and built a fort, named Fort Meigs, behind the rapids of the Maumee as an advanced base for operations against Detroit. There he lay with some thirteen hundred men, awaiting the arrival of as many more under General Clay, when Proctor conceived the project of assailing the fort before Clay's reinforcements could come up.

Accordingly on the 23rd of April he embarked at Amherstburg something over one thousand men of all ranks, half of them militia, and four hundred of the remainder taken from the Forty-First, together with a few heavy guns which had been captured at Detroit. On the 27th he landed on the north bank of the Maumee and encamped a mile and a half below Fort Meigs, which was situated on the southern bank. Here he was joined by some twelve hundred Indians under Tecumseh; but heavy rains impeded the transport of the guns, and it was only on the 1st and 2nd of May that his first batteries opened fire from the north bank.

The result was trifling; and the fire of a third battery, completed twenty-four hours later on the south bank, was little more effective, while at the same time exposing the flank companies of the Forty-First, which had been detached to guard it, to the risk of destruction in detail. Harrison was not slow to detect this blunder, and hearing at midnight of the 4th that Clay's reinforcement was within two hours' march of the fort, he directed that officer to land eight hundred men on the north bank of the river, carry the two batteries on that side, spike the guns, and then cross the river to join the rest of the force at Fort Meigs.

At the outset the movement was perfectly successful. Clay's left-hand column made a rush at the batteries at nine o'clock in the morning, and, finding them unguarded, mastered them at once; but, instead of spiking the guns and returning to their boats, the men remained where they were. A counter-attack by three companies of the Forty-First soon drove them from the captured works into the forest, where the Indians fell upon them and routed them completely. Simultaneously with Clay's attack Harrison made a sortie from the fort, surprised a party of the Forty-First and took nearly fifty of them prisoners; but the remainder—reinforced by a few militia and Indians—retook the guns and drove the enemy back with loss into their entrenchments. Altogether between four and five hundred American prisoners were taken, and some forty, despite all attempts of their escort to protect them, were massacred by the Indians. Proctor's loss did not exceed sixty-one killed or wounded and forty prisoners, which last were immediately recovered by exchange.

So far the action was a success, though it was most discreditable to Proctor that his troops on both sides of the river should have been taken by surprise. The guns on the north bank, having been imperfectly spiked by the Americans, renewed their fire; and a display of the white flag by Harrison flattered Proctor with the hope that he contemplated surrender. The crafty American, however, only wished to suspend hostilities long enough to enable him to secure the boats with supplies and stores, which had accompanied Clay; and having accomplished this he resumed his defiance.

The Indians now began to desert in hundreds. Half of the Canadian militia deserted also, and the remainder declared their determination to return home likewise. Very unwillingly Proctor found himself compelled to raise the siege, and by the 14th of May he was again at Amherstburg, having brought off all his guns and stores, but accomplished little towards the salvation of the western settlement. Looking to the general conduct of the expedition it cannot be said that he deserved success.

His position was now become exceedingly unpleasant. His force, owing to the disappearance of the militia, was reduced to a handful of men, and reinforcements, consisting of the remainder of the Forty-First which had been long promised by Prevost, had not yet reached him. He was in want of camp-equipage, of money, clothing, ammunition and flesh; and the Indians, but meagrely supplied with food, arms and presents, were beginning to waver in their allegiance.

In the middle of June he was somewhat cheered by the arrival of Captain Barclay of the Royal Navy to take command of the British squadron on Lake Erie; but that officer brought only a handful of sailors with him; and the great need of the extreme west was men. Throughout the month of June Proctor waited in vain for more regular soldiers who never came. Prevost had ordered Vincent to detach men to Proctor's assistance; but Vincent, having already a superior force of Americans before him at Fort George, was naturally unwilling to weaken himself. Barclay was equally unfortunate, for Yeo dreaded parting with any of his small body of trained sailors in the presence of Chauncey. In fact there were not men enough to defend the whole of Canada, except against so unmilitary a nation as the Americans; and even then the little detachments of British troops required handling by a master in order to ensure success.

Early in July Proctor began to realise that he had struck his blow in the wrong quarter, and that he ought to have destroyed the enemy's naval station at Fort Erie, he wrote:

> It could easily have been done a short time since, it will now be a work of difficulty . . . I would not willingly attack it without the whole of the first battalion of the Forty-first. . . . It is not too late if they were sent at once to Long Point. (on the northern shore of the lake).—Proctor to Prevost and M'Donall, 4th July 1813.

Barclay on his side renewed his entreaties for seamen, artificers and stores of all kinds. He had a new ship, the *Detroit*, nearly ready for launching, but no means of manning and equipping her; while the crews of the six ships which composed the remainder of the squadron were of the most heterogeneous description—Newfoundland soldiers, British soldiers, undisciplined Canadian boatmen, who knew not a word of English—everything in fact except sailors. (see list following).

★★★★★★

List of the Erie Fleet :

	Guns.	Canadians.	Newfound-land Regt.	Forty-first.	Total.
Queen Charlotte, ship,	16	40	25	45	110
Lady Prevost, schooner,	12	30	10	36	76
General Hunter, brig,	6	20	4	15	39
Erie, schooner,	2	6	4	5	15
Little Belt, sloop,	3	6	4	5	15
Chippewa, schooner,	2				

Prevost to Sec. of State, 20th July 1813.

The list in James's *Naval War between Great Britain and the United States* gives the *Hunter* 10 guns ; but this refers to a later period.

★★★★★★

Prevost answered by pressing de Rottenburg, who was now in

Battery of 6 pdrs

Assaulting Party
led by Lt Col Short

Ravine

Glacis

FORT
STEPHENSON

Well

Magazine

Ticket Office

Storehouse

Gate

under
Lt. Col. Warburton

Grenadiers

Line of March

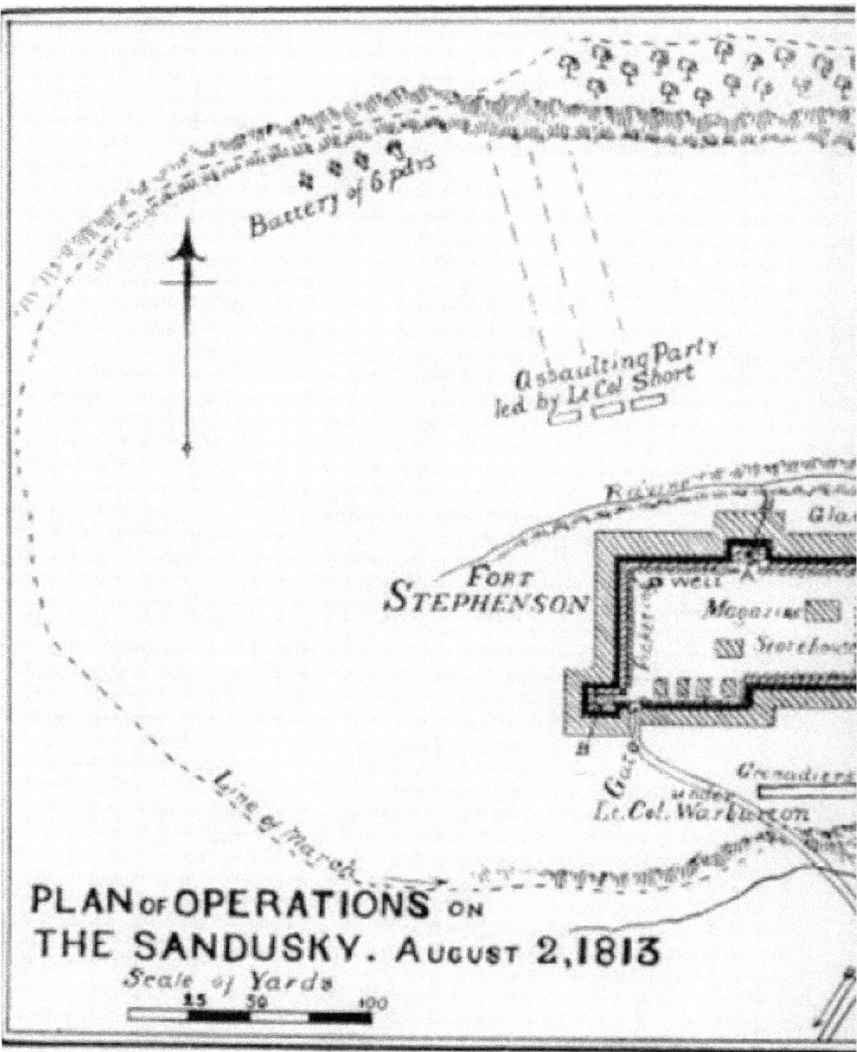

**PLAN of OPERATIONS on
THE SANDUSKY. August 2, 1813**

Scale of Yards

15   50   100

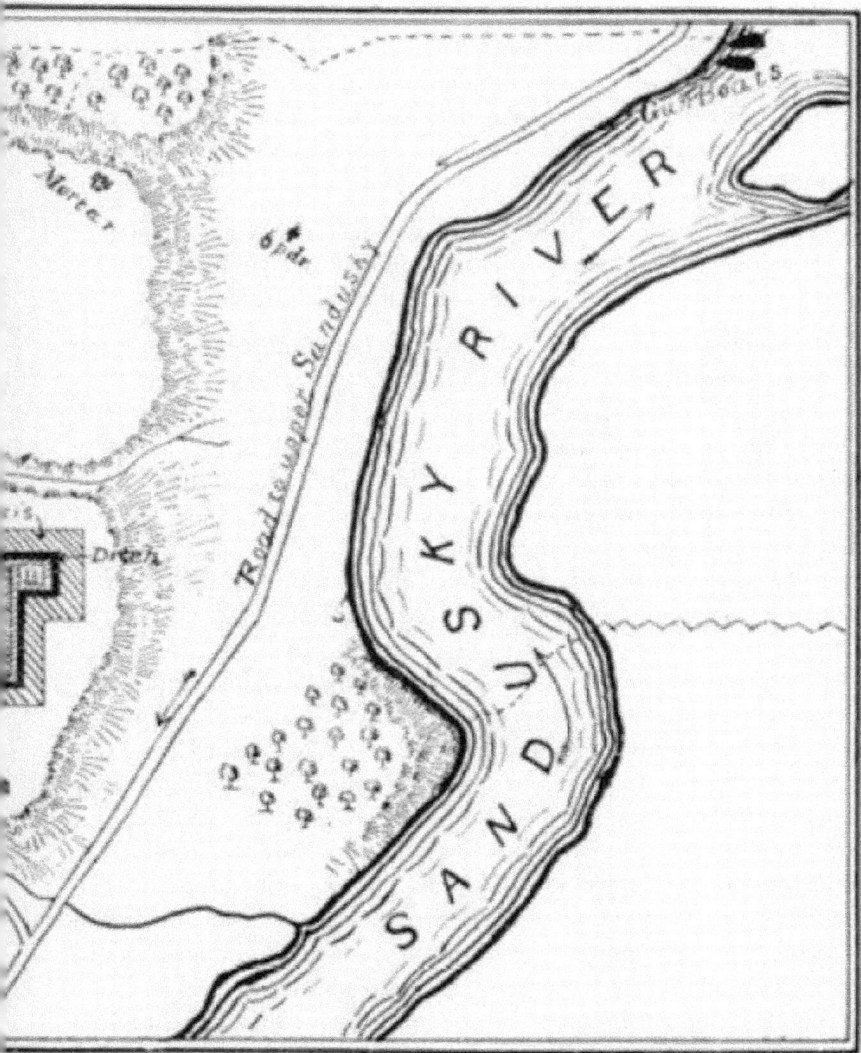

Mercer

6 Pdr.

Road to upper Sandusky

Ditch

SANDUSKY RIVER

Gunboats

command at Niagara, to send up the remainder of the first battalion of the Forty-First, promising also to despatch the second battalion besides small detachments of the Royal Scots and Hundred and Fourth. At last in the middle of July a hundred men of the Forty-First arrived at Long Point; but de Rottenburg declined to part with more troops, preferring to inform Proctor of the arrangements made for his retreat in case of a naval disaster on Lake. Erie. Proctor wrote bitterly that no doubt Prevost intended to help him, but that his good intentions were unavailing:

> Had the force ordered been sent to me I could have taken Presqu'ile (Erie), thus securing the command of the Lake. . . . If the command be lost it will be difficult to recover it.

He could only order Barclay to pick up the reinforcement at Long Point, and to proceed to the blockade of the enemy's naval base.

With a force depleted by the necessity of supplying Barclay with crews, Proctor was left mainly dependent on the Indians, who now proposed a second attack upon Fort Meigs. The design, said to have been framed by Tecumseh himself, was to decoy part of the garrison into the forest by opening a heavy fire, and to fall upon its rear as soon as it was safely entangled in the trees; whereupon the British, who were to be concealed near the fort, would endeavour to storm it by surprise.

Proctor consented to this flimsy stratagem against his better judgment, as he admitted; and accordingly towards the end of July he sailed for the Maumee with four hundred of the Forty-First and a few field-guns. Tecumseh's plan failed completely; most of the Indians returned to their homes; and Proctor, in order to keep the remnant with him, re-embarked his troops for an attack upon Fort Stephenson, the American post at Sandusky. Moving up the river in boats, he opened his attack on the evening of the 1st of August with an ineffectual bombardment; and on the evening of the 2nd, yielding once more to the importunity of the Indians, he delivered an assault.

The garrison of the place numbered no more than one hundred and sixty men with a single field-gun; but it was situated in a strong position on the lip of a deep wooded ravine, the whole being surrounded by a stockade and by an external ditch eight feet wide and as many deep. The assault was to have been delivered at two different points, the one being entrusted to the Indians and the other to the Forty-First; but neither scaling-ladders nor fascines were provided to facilitate the passage of the ditch; wherefore, though the British made their way gallantly to the bottom of it under a heavy fire, they could advance no farther, and were shot down at leisure by the Americans.

The Indians never fell on at all; and after two hours of fruitless endeavour Proctor drew off his men under cover of darkness, and, leaving the greater number of his killed and wounded—ninety-six in all—behind him, returned to the mouth of the Detroit River. The action was highly creditable to the young officer, Major Croghan, who commanded the garrison, and much the reverse to Proctor. It is difficult, perhaps, to blame a man who in so desperate a position endeavoured to conciliate his only allies, the Indians, by a desperate venture; but a commander can never be excused, least of all in a dangerous enterprise, for neglecting the most elementary means of obtaining success. His situation was doubtless trying and discouraging to the last degree; but it is very evident that Proctor had lost his temper, patience and hope, looked upon himself as sacrificed to the welfare of de Rottenburg, and was disposed to drift carelessly in what direction soever the eddies of circumstance might guide him.

Meanwhile, on the very day of the failure before Fort Stephenson, Perry had begun the most difficult and dangerous operation of bringing his vessels from their anchorage through a very shallow channel into deep water. To effect this he was obliged not only to take out the guns from the larger ships, but to lift them over the bar with floats; and it was not until the evening of the 4th that Perry could report the entire squadron as safe in deep water.

On the same day Barclay returned to the blockade and found himself too late. His new ship, the *Detroit*, had been launched, but was still unready for service; and he was obliged to return in all haste to fit her out. By one shift and another she was within the next three weeks masted and equipped, and by the disarming of Fort Amherstburg she was furnished with nineteen guns of four different calibres. (Proctor wrote to Prevost on the 26th of August that all his ordnance, except his field-guns, was on the fleet).

But she still needed to be manned, and it was difficult to say where a crew could be found for her, for there were only twenty-five British seamen on Lake Erie. Perry himself had been nearly as much embarrassed for sailors as was Barclay, for Chauncey, like Yeo, was unwilling to spare any of his own; and in fact Perry had taken the water with no more than three hundred, including a proportion of landsmen, out of a proper complement of seven hundred and forty. On the 10th of

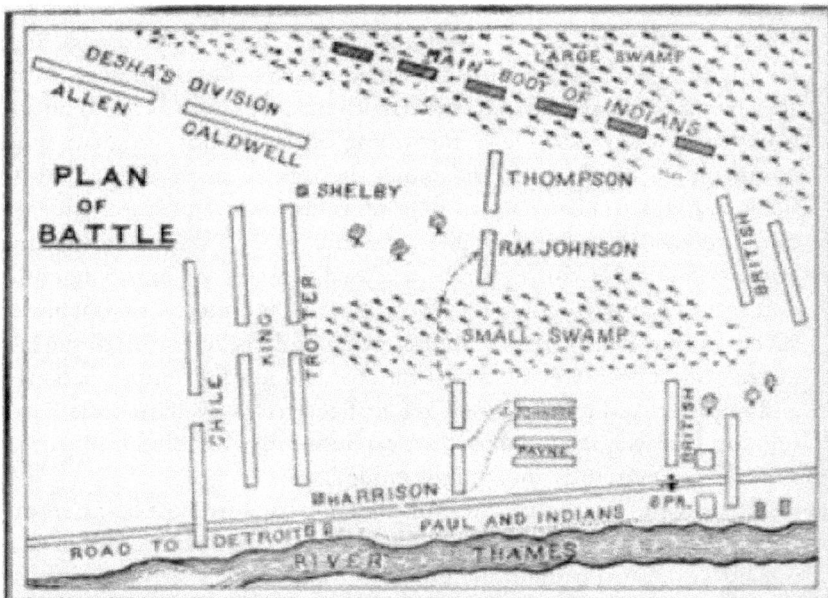

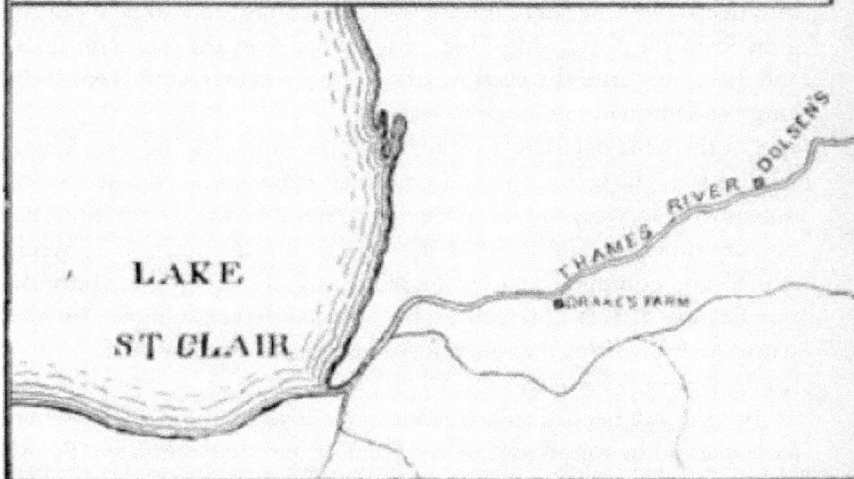

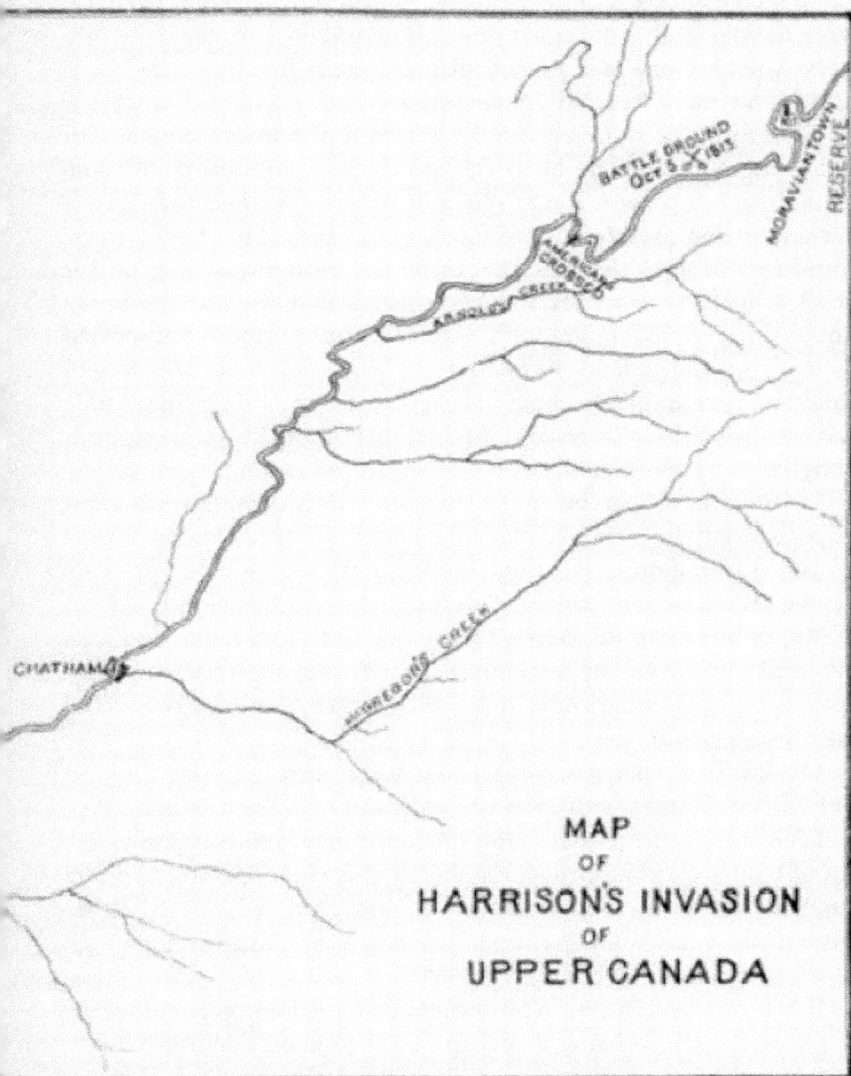

MAP
OF
HARRISON'S INVASION
OF
UPPER CANADA

BATTLE GROUND
OCT 5 1813

MORAVIANTOWN

RESERVE

INDIAN
CROSSING

ARNOLD'S CREEK

McGREGOR'S CREEK

CHATHAM

August, however, he received a reinforcement of one hundred seamen, and established his headquarters at Put-in Bay, about thirty miles to south of the mouth of the Detroit, from which point he made frequent reconnaissances of the British squadron at Amherstburg. Barclay was naturally in no condition to meet him; and Proctor stated the case fairly when he informed Prevost that, so long as Barclay was without seamen, he ought to avoid the enemy.

This, however, signified that for the time the naval command of Lake Erie was yielded to the Americans, a very serious matter. Prevost, in order to be nearer at hand to help Proctor, moved his headquarters during the third week in July to the Niagara frontier; but he acknowledged that he could do little to remedy the most threatening danger of all, namely the interception of Proctor's supplies. For the white troops alone enough might with great exertion have been transported by land; but the Indians, some fourteen thousand men, women and children, also required feeding; and the victualling of such a multitude was possible only if there were free transit for British shipping from Long Point to the River Detroit.

By the 5th of September the situation had become alarming, for there was only from two to three days' flour left, and Proctor's commissary was in despair. For three more days Barclay waited anxiously for the arrival of forty or sixty seamen, whom Prevost on the 22nd of August had reported to be on their way to Kingston; but a sudden movement of the enemy, presently to be narrated, upon Sackett's Harbour caused the commander-in-chief to return hastily eastward, and the waiting was in vain.

On the 9th, when his crews had already been for some time on half-rations, Barclay, with Proctor's approval, sailed out to meet Perry. Each squadron had two large ships, and one intermediate vessel; but of lighter craft the British numbered only three against six, while the American ships, though themselves undermanned, carried rather more men, and an infinitely larger proportion of trained seamen.

★★★★★★

Barclay indeed had only 50 seamen in a total complement of 440; the balance being made up of 250 soldiers and 140 Canadians, who could not even understand English. Perry had nominally 532 men; but it is stated that not more than 416 were fit for duty; in which case the number (allowing for a little sickness on the British side) would be about equal.

★★★★★★

Barclay's one hope was that the ordnance of his flag-ship the *Detroit*, being composed almost entirely of guns of long range, might give him the advantage over the two larger American vessels, both of which were armed mainly with carronades. But on the other hand the American small craft carried without exception heavy guns of long range, which made one of them more than a match for all three of the British. Moreover, the matches and tubes in store at Amherstburg were so defective that the only means of discharging the British guns was to fire a pistol into the vent.

Just before morning of the 10th the two squadrons met; and after a very severe action of nearly three hours' duration the entire British squadron was captured. The result was due chiefly to the skill and daring of Perry, without which his superiority of force would have been useless. Even as things were, the *Lawrence*, his flag-ship, was so much shattered that he was obliged to shift his flag to the *Niagara*, and to leave the *Lawrence* to surrender; and his losses, though far smaller in proportion to his strength than those of the British, who had one hundred and thirty-five killed and wounded, (27 killed and 96 wounded, of which 22 killed and 61 wounded belonged to the *Lawrence*), were little fewer than those of his adversary. But fortune sided against Barclay throughout. A sudden shift of wind transferred the weather-gauge from him to his adversary just before the action began, and deprived him of the advantage of choosing his own range for his cannon. He was very severely wounded, and every one of his naval officers was disabled or killed. He did all that a brave and skilful seaman could do, and worthily upheld the honour of the service.

Prevost, on receiving news of the disaster on the 22nd, ordered Proctor to retire at once to the Thames, and directed de Rottenburg to move forward his division to meet him and carry him supplies. Proctor of his own accord, before he received these instructions, made up his mind that he must destroy Forts Amherstburg and Detroit, and retreat; but, considering that his supplies had been cut off and that he had lost a third of his men and the whole of his guns in Barclay's squadron, he appears to have been amazingly dilatory in his proceedings. He must have cherished some idea of checking the Americans, for he wrote on the 15th that he still had hopes of "making them uncomfortable."

Be that as it may, it was not until the 18th that he announced his intentions to the Indians, who only with much reluctance yielded to his wishes, and not until the 24th that, having sent his baggage before

PERRY LEAVING THE *LAWRENCE*

him, he finally marched from Amherstburg northward to Sandwich, whence, having picked up the garrison of Detroit, he on the 27th turned eastward towards the Thames.

★★★★★★

As Sir C. Lucas points out (*War of 1812*), there is great confusion about the dates; but the Americans certainly crossed to Amherstburg on the 27th, which Richardson says was the third day after the British left it. On the other hand the charges against Proctor set forth that he did not really begin his retreat till the evening of the 27th.

★★★★★★

Even then his movements seem to have been something more than slow, for his force took more than a week to reach that river, halting on the 1st of October at a hamlet about fifteen miles from its mouth.

The Americans, meanwhile, had crossed the lake on the 27th, and occupied the ruins of the two forts; and at last on the 2nd of October General Harrison marched from Sandwich with from three to five thousand men in pursuit of Proctor. All through that day the British commander remained stationary; but on the 3rd, on learning of Harrison's advance, he resumed his retreat up the Thames, crossed it, and on the afternoon of the 5th halted at a point about two miles short of a missionary settlement known as Moravian Town.

Harrison, for his part, had found every inducement to hasten his march. The bridges over the tributary creeks on the lower reaches of the Thames had been left intact by Proctor. A small party of British was captured in the act of destroying one of them on the evening of the 3rd; and from that moment derelict boats and abandoned stores quickened both the zeal and the speed of the pursuers. On the morning of the 5th Harrison took two vessels loaded with stores and ammunition, together with the greater number of the party, one hundred and fifty strong, which formed their guard. At noon he passed his force across the river in such small craft as he could find; and his mounted men pressed on, carrying infantry on their horses behind them. Another ten miles brought the Americans face to face with the remains of Proctor's detachment drawn up in a position astride of the road.

The remnant now left to Proctor counted about four hundred white troops, chiefly of the Forty-First, and a rather larger number of Indians, the whole numbering, perhaps, one-fourth of the strength of their opponents. But unfortunately numerical inferiority was not the only defect on the British side, for the men were also thoroughly demoralised. During the retreat they had formed the conviction, which unhappily appears to have been justified, that their commander was more anxious for the safety of his family and his private property than of his troops. From beginning to end Proctor was always with the advanced parties, never with the rear guard.

At Moravian Town there was an excellent position on a small open plain, where the front was covered by a wooded ravine, the left flank secured by the river, and the right by a thick forest admirably adapted to the tactics of the Indians. This position it had been intended to entrench; and Proctor had actually visited it on the 3rd and placed all of his few field-guns, except one, upon it. The difficult access by the ravine would have checked the mounted infantry, over one thousand strong, which formed the most formidable part of Harrison's force. But, whether to secure the retreat of his family, or for whatever reason, Proctor kept his men for two hours in their original halting-place, two miles from Moravian Town.

Here their flanks were indeed protected by the river on their left and a marsh on their right, but the main body was withdrawn into a wood not dense enough to prevent practised horsemen from moving swiftly within it, yet sufficiently dark to make the scarlet uniforms of the British conspicuous, and to allow their enemy to approach within twenty yards of them unperceived. Moreover, no orders were given as to the disposition of the troops in the event of an attack.

Thus it came about that when the alarm was sounded the Forty-First, who were sitting at their ease on logs and fallen trees, were hustled into line without order or method. Two companies were then suddenly withdrawn to form a second line two hundred yards in rear of the first; and Proctor's solitary gun was placed on the road alongside the river under escort of a handful of Canadian dragoons, at a point where nothing was visible at a greater range than fifty yards from the muzzle.

Moreover, as though this were not folly enough, no ammunition had been brought up for the gun. Harrison, having a force of over three thousand men, decided to post his infantry so as to check any attack of the Indians on his left flank, and launched his mounted infantry straight upon the first line of the Forty-First. These received them with two volleys, but, being in extended order, were ridden down at once; and the greater number then laid down their arms without further resistance. A few fled to the shelter of the reserve, which was likewise overpowered after firing two volleys; and the mounted infantry then wheeled upon the flank of the Indians, while the American foot engaged them in front.

For a short time the Indians resisted bravely until discouraged by the fall of their leader Tecumseh, when they also broke and fled. Proctor galloped away immediately after the defeat of the first line, and, though hard pressed by the mounted Americans, succeeded in making his escape. A few of the Canadians rode with him, and one officer and some fifty men of the Forty-First contrived also to elude pursuit in the woods. The remainder of the Europeans were captured; no more than forty-eight of them having fallen under the American bullets. (Harrison in his despatch claims to have taken 601 regular British troops prisoners, this, however, comprehends all prisoners taken both in the pursuit and in the action, including at least 170 sick). The American loss did not exceed seven killed and twenty-two wounded.

Though the numerical superiority of the Americans over Proctor's whole force was at least three to one, this was a very disgraceful defeat. Proctor laid the blame on the troops, and Prevost issued a general order of scathing reprobation upon all concerned; but there could be little doubt who was really responsible for the disaster. After long but inevitable delay Proctor was tried by court-martial at Montreal in December 1814, and was found guilty of carelessness in conducting the retreat, of neglect in omitting to take up the position at Moravian Town, and of making defective dispositions to receive the American attack; but in consideration of his previous services he was sentenced only to a public reprimand and to suspension from rank and pay for six months.

The Horse Guards, however, thought with justice that the court had been too lenient, and, being unable to reassemble it, issued a general order, which was read at the head of every regiment in the army, reprimanding Proctor in terms so severe as to brand him with indelible dishonour. The truth is that he was a bad and incompetent officer, who had been saved many times from the consequences of his own incapacity by the Forty-First, and in return for their good service had so mishandled the regiment that they would work for him no longer. Had he been tried by the court which tried Whitelocke, he would certainly have been cashiered. (Richardson's *War of 1812* and Coffin's *1812*).

Thus the Americans, after two campaigns, succeeded at last in driving the British from Lake Erie, though a British, garrison still held Mackinaw and, as shall be told in place, managed to retain it until the

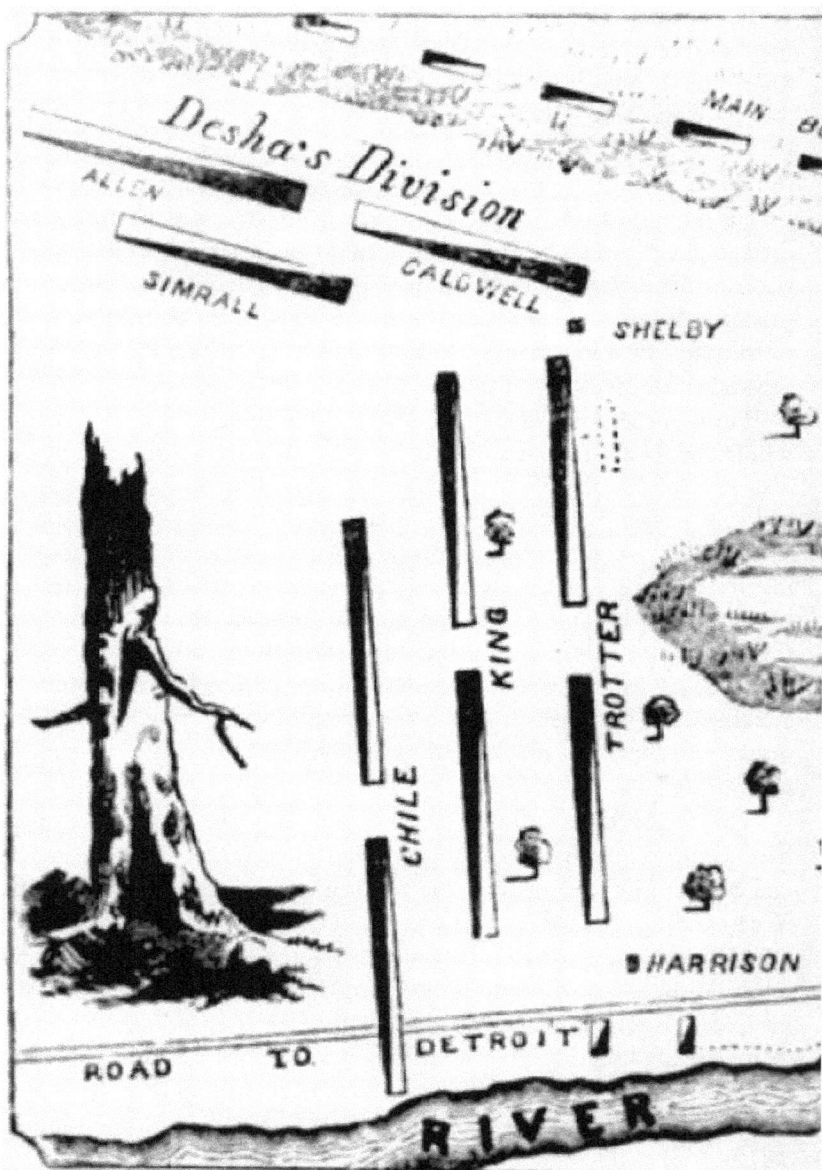

Desha's Division

ALLEN

SIMRALL

CALDWELL

SHELBY

CHILE

KING

TROTTER

HARRISON

ROAD TO DETROIT

RIVER

MAIN

BATTLE OF

THE THAMES.

end of the war. Vincent, who was in temporary charge of the troops about Niagara, heard of the action at Moravian Town on the 8th of October, and at once concentrated every man under his orders at Burlington Heights. De Rottenburg, who was on his way to Kingston, receiving exaggerated news of the mishap, sent Vincent instructions to destroy all stores and to fall back to Kingston, if he thought himself too weak to meet the superior force of the enemy.

These instructions were confirmed by Prevost, who had likewise been deceived by the narrative of a fugitive officer, but were countermanded on the 1st of November in time to prevent Vincent from moving out of his position. As a matter of fact Harrison had not followed up his victory, but had retired, not a little harassed by the Indians as he went, to Detroit, where he found fresh orders awaiting him from headquarters.

In truth the American Government was meditating a great stroke upon Kingston and Montreal, having been guided towards this very sound decision by the advice of Mr Armstrong, the Secretary for War. For some time past it had been resolved to concentrate at Sackett's Harbour all the troops from Niagara, except the garrisons of Forts George and Niagara on either side of the river; and it was now determined to add to these also part of Harrison's victorious force from the Thames.

A new commander-in-chief, General Wilkinson, had lately superseded Dearborn; Armstrong himself had taken up his residence in Sackett's Harbour at the beginning of September; and on the 9th Chauncey sailed to Niagara with his squadron to protect the embarkation of three thousand soldiers. Before these operations could be completed, the American commander heard that Yeo with his squadron was at York, and sailed out to meet him. On the 28th the two fleets met and parted after an indecisive action, Chauncey returning to Niagara, while Yeo anchored at the head of the lake under Burlington Heights.

By the 2nd of October the last of the American transports had sailed from Sackett's Harbour; and Chauncey, upon false information that Yeo had again sailed eastward, ran down the lake to cover the landing of the troops, capturing on the way six small vessels that were carrying reinforcements from York to Kingston. These were in fact part of two regiments which had sailed with de Rottenburg on the 2nd of October, and of which he brought the bulk safely into Kingston on the 16th. A week later Perry's squadron carried thirteen hundred of Harrison's men to Niagara; and the American preparations were complete.

Now, however, Armstrong abandoned the attack upon Kingston, doubting the success of the enterprise since the garrison had been so materially strengthened, and resolved to throw all his force against Montreal. General Wade Hampton, who commanded the army of Lake Champlain, was already at Chateaugai on the river of the same name, with four thousand effective infantry and a well-appointed train; and from this centre roads ran north-east to the junction of the river with the St. Lawrence, ten miles above Montreal, and westward to St. Regis, fifty miles higher up the St. Lawrence.

The season was so far advanced as to admit of no delay; and it was therefore arranged that Wilkinson's force should sail to Grenadier Island, near the outlet of Lake Ontario into the river, drop down the St. Lawrence by water, effect its junction with Hampton's at some unknown point, and then proceed to the attack. Chauncey was of course called upon to accompany Wilkinson, enter the St. Lawrence with his squadron, and leave Sackett's Harbour, denuded of all but a very weak garrison, to take its chance. If the British succeeded in beating either of the two columns before they could unite, the enterprise was bound to fail; and if, as Chauncey feared, Yeo chose to attack Sackett's Harbour while the American squadron was in the river, there was every prospect that the American naval base would be destroyed.

Altogether the great plan, originally conceived upon perfectly sound principles, had degenerated into something radically vicious. The American generals were at great pains to make the worst of a bad design. On the 21st Hampton broke up his camp, and marched down the Chateaugai. Having driven in a picquet of Canadian militia at the junction of the Outard and Chateaugai Rivers on the 22nd, he halted there for three days to repair the road and bring forward his artillery. This done he opened a line of communication with Ogdensburg, about eighty-five miles up the St. Lawrence, so as to keep in touch with Wilkinson, and matured his scheme for an attack upon Prevost's advanced posts.

According to his information there was nothing on his immediate front but three hundred Canadian fencibles and voltigeurs, with a party of Indians, under Lieutenant-Colonel de Salabery; and he therefore arranged that his main body should advance down the left bank of the Chateaugai to the forest where de Salabery was known to be lying, and engage him in front, while a detached column under Colonel

Purdy was to move down the right bank, seize a ford some ten miles down, and recross in rear of him. Purdy marched on the night of the 25th, and was no sooner gone past recall than a messenger came in from Wilkinson to say that it was impossible for him yet to co-operate in the movement. However it was now too late to countermand it, and on the 26th Hampton advanced at the head of his main body.

Between ten and eleven o'clock in the morning both columns were perceived by de Salabery's scouts, though Purdy's, having lost its way in the forest, was still far in rear. Prevost, having warning of the American advance, had summoned a newly raised battalion under Lieutenant-colonel Macdonell from Kingston to the Chateaugai; and that able and energetic officer, by great exertions and at considerable risk, had carried his men down the St. Lawrence by water in the teeth of a gale, and brought them up through the forest to the rendezvous by the morning of the 25th.

De Salabery for his part knew his work, and had taken every pre-caution. He had selected a point on the road about six miles above the confluence of the Chateaugai with the St. Lawrence, where his left was protected by the former river, and his right covered by ravines, which he had further strengthened by abatis. The weak point of the position was the ford already mentioned, in its rear; but to secure this Macdonell had hidden his battalions at its outlet on the left bank, sending also, with excellent judgment, a detached company across the river to the right bank.

Purdy's three battalions blundering down to the ford early in the afternoon were staggered by a sudden volley at close range from Mac-donell's men. They appear to have rallied, however, and to have fought fairly well for a time; but Macdonell's company being reinforced by another, which engaged them from a different direction, the Ameri-cans became flurried with the noise and smoke, and began a furi-ous fight among themselves. Thereupon the Canadians quietly slipped back over the ford to the left bank, leaving the Americans to settle their differences in their own way.

Simultaneously, upon hearing the sound of musketry, Hampton launched his infantry forward against de Salabery's abatis, and suc-ceeded in driving the voltigeurs from an advanced work; but Mac-donell, seeing that there was no occasion for his men to wait longer by the ford, came up to de Salabery's support, and Hampton, on hearing the cheers of the approaching Canadians, hesitated to press the attack. Soon afterwards he learnt of the utter discomfiture of Purdy's column, and calling off his soldiers, retreated.

The whole affair was little more than a short skirmish. Not above four hundred Canadians were engaged, and their losses did not exceed twenty killed and wounded. The American loss, though heavier, was still trifling in proportion to their numbers. Yet the action was sufficient to turn Hampton back in discouragement and despair. And let it be noted that this was wholly a Canadian victory. No Englishman was present except the general and his staff; and Prevost bore eloquent testimony to the skill of the Canadian officers and to the steadiness and gallantry of the men.

Thus one of the invading columns had been successfully stopped; and the other was destined to give little more trouble than the first. After many delays owing to rough weather Wilkinson's troops were assembled at Grenadier Island by the end of October, and on the 1st of November they began to descend the river by detachments to French Creek, Chauncey bringing his squadron forward to fend off that of Yeo.

As French Creek was a point which might well indicate an attack upon Kingston, de Rottenburg made no movement; but on the night of the 5th the Americans, being all concentrated, began their passage down the river; and Wilkinson on the following night wrote to Hampton to announce his coming, and to order that the two columns should unite at St. Regis. Hampton received the letter on the night of the 7th, and answered in a lugubrious strain, setting forth the fatigue, sickliness and discouragement of his troops, also his want of supplies, and intimating that, in his view, he should afford his colleague better help by retiring to the main depot at Plattsburg, and threatening the flank of the British from that point.

Moreover, though junior to Wilkinson, he not only expressed his opinion but acted upon it, for on the 11th he calmly turned his back on St. Regis, and marched back to Lake Champlain, leaving his colleague to shift for himself. Unaware of this proceeding, Wilkinson continued his movement down the river, landing his troops at Ogdensburg, and sending the boats down by night with muffled oars, so as to avoid the guns of a small British fort at Prescott. (According to Prevost's despatch the flotilla was observed and cannonaded from Prescott; but little harm appears to have been done).

On the following morning he re-embarked his army, setting some twelve hundred men ashore on the Canadian bank to sweep away any opposition; and on the 9th the whole armament reached the head of the Long Sault rapids, at the foot of which, nine miles below, lay the appointed rendezvous of St. Regis.

But meanwhile de Rottenburg had not been idle. No sooner was he assured of the true intention of Wilkinson than, pursuant to Prevost's orders, he sent from Kingston a detachment of the Forty-Ninth and Eighty-Ninth, in all about six hundred men with two guns, under Lieutenant-Colonel Morrison, to hang upon the American rear; the whole being escorted by a small flotilla of gun-boats under Captain Mulcaster. On the 8th they picked up two more companies of the Forty-Ninth and a few Canadians—in all about two hundred men— with another field-gun, and on the 9th continued their march, the soldiers by land and the sailors by water, finally gaining contact with the enemy at the head of the rapids on the 10th.

The movements of Wilkinson had not, in fact, been speedy. He had landed General Brown with about two thousand men on the Canadian shore, and then had advanced down the bank on the 10th; but at the foot of the rapids, on the Canadian side, was the little town of Cornwall, held by a small party of militia under an officer of the Forty-Ninth, who broke down the bridges, skirmished with the advanced guard, and made himself generally so obstructive that Brown was unable to report that the rapids were clear of the enemy until the 11th.

Meanwhile, Wilkinson, painfully aware that a British force was following him and "teasing his rear" (to use his own expression), landed about eighteen hundred more men under General Boyd on the Canadian shore. On the morning of the 11th he received the welcome message from Brown, and gave the order for his boats to shoot the rapids. He had hardly done so before Mulcaster's gun-boats opened fire upon the flotilla, while Boyd reported from the shore that the British troops were pressing in upon his rear-guard. To this Wilkinson replied, as was natural and right, that Boyd must turn and attack the British at once.

Morrison, observing Boyd's preparations, took up a position near Chrystler's Farm, a building about thirty-five miles above Cornwall, occupying about seven hundred yards of open ground between the river, which protected his right, and a pine-wood, on which he rested his left. With good judgment he formed his little force in an echelon of three divisions. The flank companies of the Forty-Ninth with one gun were in advance on the right; three companies of the Eighty-Ninth with another gun, stationed to the left rear of these flank companies, formed the centre; and the main body with a third gun stood in the left rear of all, with the Indians and Canadians concealed in the wood.

Boyd, whose strength was just about double that of Morrison—eighteen hundred against nine hundred—attacked first the left flank of the British, but was promptly repulsed by the wheel of Morrison's centre division upon his left flank. He then directed fresh troops against the right flank of the British, but was again repelled in the same fashion; whereupon Morrison took the offensive, and fairly drove the Americans back in disorder, capturing one of their guns. The action was stubbornly contested for two hours, and cost the British twenty-two killed, one hundred and forty-seven wounded, and twelve missing; the Forty-Ninth—a mere fragment of a battalion—having sixty-three casualties. Of the Americans over three hundred were killed and wounded, and over one hundred taken prisoners. At the close of the engagement Morrison occupied Boyd's original position, and the American infantry pursued its way down the river, the infantry in boats, the cavalry and artillery by land, with the British still hanging closely to their skirts.

On the following day the American flotilla passed down the rapids; and Wilkinson, arrived at Cornwall, received Hampton's letter announcing his retreat to Plattsburg. Outwardly very indignant, Wilkinson submitted the situation to a Council of War, which agreed that it was expedient to abandon the advance upon Montreal for the present; and in accordance with this resolution he transferred his army on the 13th to the American shore, and entrenched himself for the winter at French Mills on the Salmon River, about eight miles east of St. Regis.

As to the impropriety, to say the least, of Hampton's conduct, there can hardly be two opinions; but to judge from the alacrity with which Wilkinson seized the pretext for abruptly ending the operations, he was probably very grateful in his secret heart to Hampton for supplying him with it. The truth is that as military leaders both men were equally incompetent.

Thus ridiculously terminated the American invasion of Lower Canada. Chauncey's squadron returned unmolested to its base on the nth, and from thence sailed to Niagara in order to bring to Sackett's Harbour the detachment of Harrison's army which had been landed on the peninsula by Perry. This was accomplished by the 21st; and by the first week in December frost compelled both naval squadrons to be laid up for the winter. The whole campaign of 1813 seemed to be finished; but, as the Americans presently discovered, the end was not

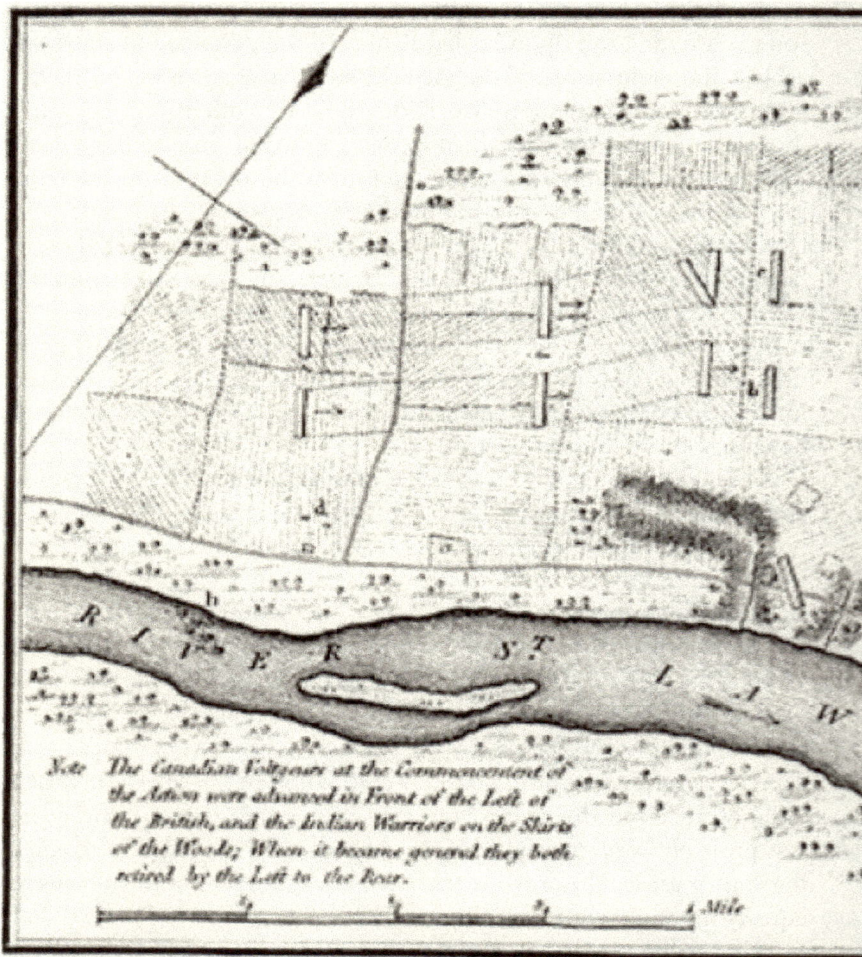

Note   The Canadian Voltigeurs at the Commencement of the Action were advanced in Front of the Left of the British, and the Indian Warriors on the Skirts of the Woods; When it became general they both retired by the Left to the Rear.

R I V E R   S T.   L A W

Mile

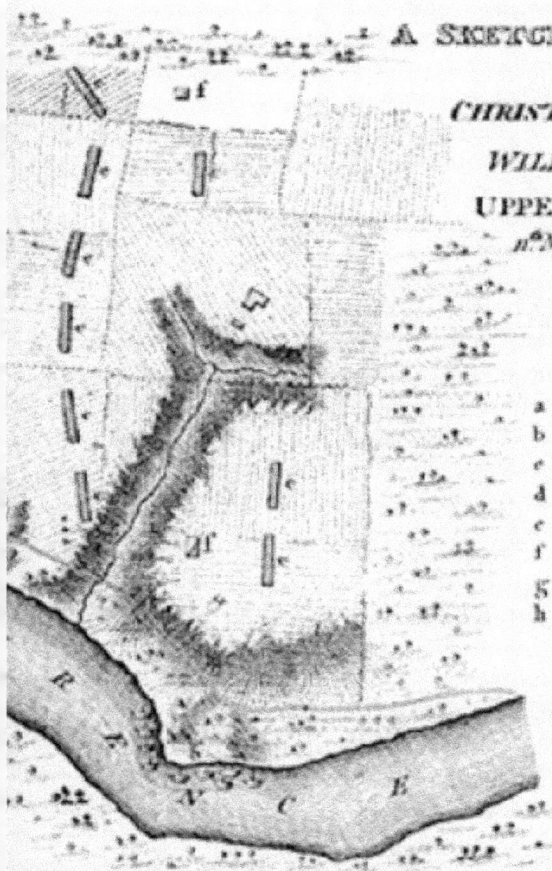

A SKETCH of the BATTLE
at
CHRISTLERS FARM
WILLIAMSBURG
UPPER CANADA
11ᵗʰ Novᵣ 1813.

References.

a Corps of Detachments
b 49ᵗʰ Regᵗ
c 89ᵗʰ Regᵗ
d Christlers Farm
e American Infantry
f .... Cavalry
g .... Gun Boats
h British Gun Boats

yet. Upon the removal of Harrison's troops from Niagara that general, never doubting that Wilkinson would advance triumphantly to Montreal, instructed his successor, Brigadier M'Clure, that the bulk of the British troops would be concentrated at Kingston, with no doubt a garrison at York, but with no outpost farther to the west, excepting possibly a small detachment at Burlington Heights.

Herein Harrison was deceived, for, though de Rottenburg had withdrawn from Vincent the Forty-Ninth, he had left with him the Hundredth Foot besides the relics of the Forty-First which had escaped from Moravian Town; and Vincent had no intention of retiring. Ignorant of Vincent's strength, M'Clure remained at Twenty Mile Creek with about a thousand militia, who, as the time of their service approached its end, took leave of all semblance of discipline, robbed and plundered in all directions, and, by their commander's own admission, became utterly ungovernable.

At the end of November, however, Vincent sent forward a detachment under Colonel Murray, which pushed the Americans steadily back into Fort George; and at length on the 9th of December the whole of the militiamen dispersed to their homes, leaving M'Clure with no more than sixty regular troops and forty volunteers. On the night of the 10th, therefore, he evacuated Fort George, and presently retired with his guns and stores across the river to Fort Niagara. But he could not execute even this simple manoeuvre without first burning from mere wantonness the village of Newark, and driving four hundred women and children from their homes into the snows of a Canadian winter.

On the 12th Murray occupied Fort George; and a few days later the command in Upper Canada was taken over by Lieutenant-general Gordon Drummond, who had just arrived from England. He was an officer who had seen campaigns in the West Indies and in Egypt, and had already served for three years on the staff in Canada. Upon arrival in his government on the 13th, he at once proceeded to Fort George, where Murray laid before him a plan for an attack upon Fort Niagara. This plan he approved; and, there being but two boats on the spot, several more were brought overland with incredible labour from Burlington Bay, and successfully launched on the Niagara River.

The grenadier company of the Royal Scots, the flank companies of the Forty-First, and the whole of the Hundredth, (Drummond's account says that only the flank companies of the 100th were present; but Murray's report shows that the whole regiment took part in the attack), together with a small detachment of artillery—in all rather over one thousand of all ranks—were placed under Murray's command, who took them over the water on the night of the 18th, and landed about three miles above the fort.

Two outlying picquets of the Americans were surprised and bayoneted to a man before they could give the alarm; the sentries on the glacis were likewise surprised, and the password was extorted from them; and at five o'clock on the morning of the 19th the little detachment without firing a shot fell upon the fort, the main body rushing in by the main gate when it was opened for relief of the guard, while a small party escaladed the eastern *demi*-bastion. In half an hour the British were in possession of the place at the cost of no more than six killed and five wounded. Sixty-five of the Americans were killed, and three hundred and fifty-eight of all ranks taken prisoners, of whom fourteen only were wounded. Twenty-seven guns and large quantities of arms, ammunition, stores and clothing fell also into the hands of Drummond, a very acceptable capture at the opening of a winter campaign.

On the same day Drummond followed up his success by detaching the rest of the Royal Scots and the Forty-First, in company with a large number of Indians, under Major-General Riall, (just arrived from England), against the American fort at Lewiston, which was abandoned by the enemy on their approach, together with two guns and a quantity of provisions.

Lewiston itself, Fort Schlosser, and several other villages were burned in revenge for the wanton destruction of Newark; and Riall continued his march up the river to within ten miles of Buffalo, where, being stopped by a broken bridge, he recrossed the river to Queenston. M'Clure, who had by chance shifted his quarters to Buffalo just before the storm of Fort Niagara, wrote a wild letter about the "horrid slaughter" on this occasion, but reported that he had called out the militia and that Buffalo was safe.

Very fortunately for him he was now relieved of his command by Major-General Hall, or he would speedily have found out his mistake. Drummond, always energetic and stimulated to redoubled activity by the outrages of M'Clure's militiamen, on the 28th moved his head-quarters up the river to Chippewa; and on the night of the 29th he sent Riall again across the water with about eleven hundred white troops (Royal Scots, 370; 4 cos. 8th, 240; 41st, 250; light cos. 89th, 55; grenadier cos. 100th, 50; militia volunteers, 50. Total, 1025; rank and file, say

1100 of all ranks), and four hundred Indians to attack the American posts at Black Rock and Buffalo. By midnight all, except four hundred of the Royal Scots, had disembarked two miles below Black Rock; and the leading company presently surprised an American picquet, capturing most of the men and securing the bridge, which had been prepared for destruction, over a creek that barred the way.

As soon as Riall's party had been safely disembarked, the Royal Scots began to drag their boats upstream to the foot of the rapids below Fort Erie, intending to cross from that point, land in rear of the enemy's position and cut off their retreat. Unfortunately, owing to the darkness, the boats were brought up to a shallow beach, where they grounded, and the enemy discovering them opened a heavy fire. Five field-guns posted by Drummond on the Canadian side promptly answered them, but with no great effect; and, though by great exertions the boats were shoved off, it was daylight before the Royal Scots reached the American shore, having suffered not a little both from musketry and cannonade while stationary and on passage.

Quickened by the sound of the firing, Riall left two companies to guard the captured bridge and advanced with all haste upon Black Rock. The Americans were strongly posted, and a few brave disciplined men among them defended their entrenchments with obstinacy for a time; but at length they were driven from their batteries and pursued to Buffalo, where they attempted to make another stand. Their efforts were in vain; and presently the whole broke and fled into the forest, leaving altogether eight guns, heavy and light, in the hands of the British.

Three vessels of the lake-squadron were found ashore just below the town, and were burned. Buffalo was burned likewise with all its stores, there being no means of removing them. Black Rock was burned, and every remaining American settlement on the river was destroyed. The whole of the frontier, in fact, was laid in ashes as reprisal for the burning of Newark. The operations cost the British ninety-eight killed and wounded, more than half of whom belonged to the Royal Scots. The loss of the Americans can hardly have been less, and they left one hundred and thirty prisoners in Riall's hands. They acknowledged that they had two thousand men present; but two-thirds of these were militiamen who made no effort to stand by their gallant comrades of the regular army. This sufficiently accounts for the weakness of the American resistance.

Drummond now placed his troops in winter quarters; and the

campaign of 1813, chequered by many vicissitudes, came to an end. The only substantial gain to the Americans was the destruction of Barclay's fleet on Lake Erie; for the British had reconquered the lost peninsula of Niagara, and indeed they held Fort Niagara, on American territory, for the rest of the war. The appearance of Drummond in fact came as a welcome change after the wretched mediocrity of leadership which for the most part had impartially characterised both sides; and it is more than ever evident that, if Brock had been spared, the American operations in the west would have been one long series of disgraces, which even the gallantry and enterprise of Perry would have been unable to avert.

The destruction of Newark by M'Clure and the reprisals which inevitably followed upon it were most unfortunate incidents which greatly embittered the contest, and all the more because of Drummond's acknowledgment that, in spite of all his endeavours, he was powerless to prevent some shameful outrages by Indians. The Americans of course had no one but themselves to thank for this. The Indians had suffered many injuries from them, and had many cruel wrongs to avenge. It was impossible for the tribes to remain neutral; and it was practically certain that they would favour the British, whom they liked, rather than the Americans, whom they hated.

The Government of the United States should have considered all this before invading Canada, but young democracies are always thoughtless, especially when greed of territory is in question. If, as they had expected and indeed as they ought, the Americans had marched into Quebec within two months of the declaration of war, the Indians would have given little trouble, and would have hastened to make their peace with the victors. As things were, the American troops and leaders, with some few brilliant exceptions, proved themselves so contemptible that in two full years they accomplished absolutely nothing. The Indians as the allies of the more successful party had the advantage of avenging themselves upon their enemies, and naturally would not be hindered from seizing it, while the Americans, as naturally, fiercely resented the sufferings of their kith and kin at the hands of savages.

In truth war, an ugly thing at the best of times, is rarely so inhuman as when waged by amateurs. It is difficult enough to keep disciplined men in hand when flushed by victory or discouraged by defeat; but with undisciplined men and untrained leaders the task is impossible. Under generals so helpless, nerveless and shiftless as Dearborn,

Wilkinson, Hampton and M'Clure the American militiaman, with all the material in him to make a grand fighting man, became too often a skulking marauder; while more competent officers were paralysed because the troops entrusted to them were a mere rabble. The officers, where they did not fall to the same level as their men, found vent for their feelings in the exchange of recrimination; and the men indemnified themselves for the discomfort of service by plunder and wanton destruction of property.

Reprisals followed as a natural consequence, and the unfortunate settlers blamed the Indians, the British and their own generals for what was really the fault of the American Government or, more truly, of the ignorant democracy which inspired its action. But democracies, whether American or British, have short memories, and no love for the lessons of history. The only quality that never fails them is conceit, and the only teacher that can prevail with them is disaster.

CHAPTER 3

1814

At the close of 1813 the Americans could place to their credit one substantial gain, the destruction of Captain Barclay's fleet upon Lake Erie. This the British had countered on land by the reconquest of the whole of the lost peninsula of Niagara and the capture of Fort Niagara on the American frontier. Thereby they acquired the absolute control of the harbour of refuge where the River Niagara enters Lake Ontario, and a fortress lying on the flank of any American force that might attempt the invasion of Canada. The winter of 1813-14 was unusually mild and open, which practically frustrated all operations on both sides, owing to the extreme difficulty of transport by land in the absence of frozen snow.

In January Drummond proposed to march seventeen hundred men by land from the Niagara frontier to Detroit, cross Lake Erie on the ice to Put in Bay Island, and seize the two English prizes *Detroit* and *Queen Charlotte* which had been taken by Perry and left in that anchorage. The plan was a sound one, and would have redressed the balance of naval power on Lake Erie in England's favour; but it proved to be impossible of execution because the water was still unfrozen. On the American side for the same reason as little was done. Wilkinson on the 13th of February broke up the cantonments in which he had remained since his ridiculous campaign of 1813, and divided his force into three parts, two of which took up quarters at Plattsburg and Burlington upon Lake Champlain, and the third under General Brown went to Sackett's Harbour. He was followed up in his retreat by a small British column, which captured from him a hundred sleigh-loads of supplies and stores.

Throughout the early months of the new year Prevost petitioned earnestly for reinforcements. His best regiments had been reduced by heavy losses to comparative inefficiency; and a promise, which had been given to him in August, that three new battalions would arrive early in the spring, seemed likely to be empty of effect, since its fulfilment depended upon the arrival of troops from the West Indies after they had been relieved from England. Moreover, the reinforcements last sent to Prevost were of inferior quality, being composed of convicts from the hulks and other undesirable characters, who deserted in numbers when good opportunity offered. In the circumstances he had decided to summon the second battalion of the Eighth Foot to march over land from Fredericton, New Brunswick, to Quebec, a distance of from three to four hundred miles, which the men traversed on snow-shoes through intense cold and occasional violent storms, arriving at the beginning of March in a condition which called forth high compliments from the general.

At length in the same month the Americans opened their new campaign. Mr. Armstrong, the Secretary for War, anticipated, not without reason, that Prevost intended if possible to re-establish himself on Lake Erie, though Sir George could not hope to do so without unduly weakening the garrison either of Kingston or of Montreal. Armstrong's perfectly correct view was that the principal effort of the Northern army should be directed against one or other of these two points, so as to sever communication between Upper and Lower Canada; and, though he had been persuaded to deviate from this plan in the previous year, he was now resolved to execute it.

On the 20th of February therefore he sent two sets of instructions to General Brown at Sackett's Harbour. The one, which was intended to come to the knowledge of the British, directed that the general should move with two thousand men by way of Batavia to Buffalo, in order to recover Fort Niagara. The other, which was strictly secret, prescribed that he should march across the ice and endeavour to surprise Kingston, the garrison of which was said, probably with correctness, to have dwindled to twelve hundred men. Misunderstanding the purport of Armstrong's orders and judging himself too weak to attack Kingston, Brown marched sixty miles towards Batavia, and then seized with misgiving, hurried back to Sackett's Harbour, consulted Commodore Chauncey as to Armstrong's true meaning, and on his advice returned again to Buffalo.

The incident would not be worth the chronicling, had not Brown's movements inspired General Wilkinson with a spurious activity. Though Wilkinson was Brown's senior officer, Armstrong had given him no hint of his subordinate's operations; but, on hearing of them by common report, Wilkinson judged it his duty to make a diversion in Brown's favour. Accordingly on the 19th of March he advanced northward from Plattsburg with three thousand men to the River Lacolle, where the British had converted a stone mill into a fortified post. Arriving before this petty stronghold on the 30th, he detached six hundred men to cut off the retreat of the garrison, and opened fire upon it from three field-guns.

Greatly to his surprise the defenders, one company of the Thirteenth under Major Handcock, and another of Canadians, showed no disposition to run away. On the contrary, being reinforced by the flank companies of the Thirteenth and another company of Canadians, Handcock actually took the offensive and charged the American guns. He was twice repulsed, but stoutly maintained his position till evening, when Wilkinson turned his back upon the British and solemnly retreated to Plattsburg. The casualties of Handcock's gallant little party barely exceeded sixty, of which forty-two fell upon the grenadier company of the Thirteenth alone.

Wilkinson's losses were heavier, though slight; but so ludicrous a failure as his was too much even for the Americans. (Edgar, in *Ten Years in Upper Canada*, states them circumstantially at 13 killed, 123 wounded and 30 missing. Mahan gives the figure at over 70, which is more likely to be correct). He was removed from his command, and succeeded by General Izard.

So far, though Armstrong had indicated the right line of operations, little had been done towards pursuing it; and as it chanced, affairs on the British side were equally in a state of paralysis. Failing supplies made marine supremacy on Lake Ontario more than ever necessary for them; and Drummond, who had from the first been eager for an attack upon Sackett's Harbour, pressed for the project with increased energy in April.

Owing to greater rapidity in building new vessels, Commodore Yeo's squadron was at the moment superior to that of Chauncey, who recognised the fact with no small anxiety. Four thousand troops, however, were the fewest that could be employed against Sackett's Harbour with any hope of success, and this number was greater than Prevost was able, or at any rate willing, to spare. Prevost, as it seems to me, was wrong, for the capture of the American naval base on Lake Ontario would have disorganised all the arrangements of the enemy; and an object of such supreme importance was worth a great effort and the running of unusual risks.

Baulked of his purpose, Drummond decided to turn his expedition against Oswego, where, owing to the mildness of the winter, large quantities of guns and munitions had been accumulated by water to await transport to Sackett's. Chauncey, however, had taken the precaution of detaining the cannon and equipment in a safe place twelve miles up the Oswego River; and, the Americans having got wind of Drummond's intentions, Brown, who had again returned to Sackett's, detached three hundred men to reinforce the garrison of Oswego.

On the 3rd of May Drummond and Yeo embarked something over a thousand men, (6 cos. of Watteville's, 1 co. of Glengarry L.I.; 1 batt. of Marines; det. of artillery), at Kingston; and, after some delay through variable winds and gales, a few marines, the flank companies of Watteville's, and the light company of the Glengarries were landed under a heavy fire from the British men-of-war.

The guns of Oswego received them with a heavy cannonade; but in ten minutes the fort was stormed, the garrison as they retired up the river sinking three heavy guns and a quantity of naval stores. Seven heavy guns, besides four of lighter calibre, were taken, together with some ammunition, and the British returned to Kingston with their trophies two small schooners, two thousand barrels of provisions, and a quantity of cordage all gained at a cost of ninety-five killed and wounded. ·

This, so far as it went, was well; though owing to Chauncey's foresight, the object of the expedition had been only half accomplished. Still, the heavy cannon that were required for Chauncey's new ships could only be moved by water to Sackett's Harbour, and Yeo used all his skill in distributing his squadron so as to intercept them. Chauncey, therefore, caused the guns to be placed in *bateaux* which could creep along the coast from creek to creek, with a small force of riflemen and Indians following them afloat and ashore to defend them if they should be compelled to take refuge from attack in any inlet.

On the 28th of May these *bateaux* dropped down the river to Oswego, and in the night began their voyage northward on the lake. By noon, (May 29th), the little fleet had reached Big Sandy Creek, only eight miles distant from its ultimate destination at Stony Creek, from whence the guns could be drawn overland into Sackett's. Here the *bateaux* entered the river and anchored two miles from its mouth to await information; but two of their number were missing, having wandered away in the dark and been captured by the British small craft which

were patrolling the coast. The officer, Commander Popham, in charge
of these last, on learning from his prisoners what was going forward,
collected three gun vessels and four smaller boats, manned them with
two hundred seamen and marines, and at daylight of the 30th entered
Big Sandy Creek, having landed parties upon either bank to secure
his flanks. (Mr. Lucas describes the advance of these parties as made
in a somewhat foolhardy fashion. On the contrary Popham seems to
have taken every possible precaution consistent with the weakness of
his force).

The American commander, Captain Woolsey, who had been duly
warned of their coming, was able to conceal superior forces on the
flanks of the advancing British, which closing in upon their rear cut off
every man that was ashore. After losing over forty killed and wounded,
the remainder of the British marines and seamen, seeing that resistance was hopeless, surrendered. The affair was in itself a petty one; but
its results were great, for they ensured to Chauncey the armament
for his new ships, and therewith the certainty of being able to meet
the British squadron, for a time at any rate, with equal and, indeed,
superior strength. Popham was tried by court-martial, but was rightly
acquitted, for so great an object as that which he sought was worth the
great risk which he accepted.

Yeo, however, finding his scanty complements diminished by two
hundred good men, was furious. He decided to abandon the blockade
of Sackett's Harbour, and to stand on the defensive pending the com-
pletion of a new ship of one hundred and two guns, which was already
building and would assure him naval superiority. June was now come,
and the government of the United States at length formulated its plan
of campaign for the summer. Once again it was decided to make the
principal effort in Upper Canada, against Mackinaw and the Niagara
Peninsula, instead of against Kingston and Montreal. How Secretary
Armstrong was induced to abandon his own correct strategical views
does not appear. He combated at least the project of wasting force
upon Mackinaw, when the capture of York, which was the object of
the expedition on the Niagara frontier, would in itself cut off and reduce the distant fort on Lake Huron; but he eventually submitted to
the superior ignorance of his colleagues.

It was therefore determined that five thousand troops and three
thousand volunteers under Brown should, under protection of part of
the Erie squadron, be landed on the north coast of the lake between
Fort Erie and Long Point, some eighty miles to west of it, and advance

northward against Burlington Heights, so as to sever the British communications between their forts on the Niagara and York. The rest of the Erie squadron was to escort an armament of about a thousand men to Mackinaw. As subsidiary operations General Izard was to make a diversion against Montreal from Plattsburg; and fifteen armed boats, supported by posts from Izard's army, were to interrupt the passage by water between Kingston and Montreal. Thus the object which should have been primary was made secondary, and that which should have been secondary was made primary, according to the approved practice of the amateur strategist.

Prevost for his part had both in March and May been dabbling in negotiations for an armistice, hoping no doubt to suspend hostilities pending the termination of the war in Europe, which event might dispose the United States to agree to an amicable settlement. The idea did not commend itself to Yeo, who was consulted by Prevost, nor to the British Government, which did not receive any report of the proceedings until after the conclusion of the Peninsular War; but, as Sir George's efforts came to nothing, there is no object in dwelling further upon them. Meanwhile it must be noted that no reinforcements reached Prevost until June, when they began to arrive from various quarters; the Sixteenth and two companies of artillery from Cork at the beginning of the month; the Nineteenth from the West Indies; and the Sixth and Eighty-Second from the Peninsular Army at the end of June. Prevost had been so often disappointed over the coming of promised succours that he could not divine what force would be at his disposal for the coming campaign, and was compelled to be cautious in his dispositions.

Drummond, confidently expecting that Niagara would again be the centre of operations, begged urgently for reinforcements; and, though ultimately he proved to be correct, Prevost not unreasonably did not share his opinion. In two successive years the Americans had undoubtedly committed the blunder of attacking at the wrong point, but there could be no certainty that they would repeat this folly for a third time. On the contrary, since they had been steadily purging away incompetent commanders ever since the beginning of the war, it was to be apprehended that they might have hit upon a capable general at last; and there could be no doubt as to the military policy that would commend itself to such a man.

Be that as it may, Prevost was in no position to reinforce Upper Canada until the middle of July; and indeed the difficulties of supply

LAKE ERIE

in the exhausted province of Ontario were such that a general might well have hesitated to pour new troops into it. In addition to the soldiers there were some three thousand Indians, who had retreated with Proctor, and several hundred homeless refugees to be fed, insomuch that the rations issued to non-combatants were thrice as many as the numbers of the armed force.

By dint of great personal exertions and much journeying between York and Kingston Drummond contrived to fill the mouths, both useful and useless, that depended upon him; but at the opening of July his whole force from York on Lake Ontario to Long Point on Lake Erie did not greatly exceed four thousand men. Of these over one thousand were at York itself; seven to eight hundred were in Fort Niagara; eighteen to nineteen hundred at Fort George, Queenston, Chippewa and Fort Erie; something under three hundred at Long Point; and four to five hundred at the important connecting station of Burlington Heights. A great many men were on the sick list through fever and ague, owing to excessive fatigue and exposure.

Brown was not much better off than Drummond in the matter of men. His five thousand regulars and three thousand volunteers had dwindled to a nominal total of something less than five thousand white men of all descriptions, of whom thirty-five hundred were fit for duty, and six hundred Indians. His regular soldiers, however, had for some months past been carefully trained by competent officers, and were greatly superior to any American troops that had hitherto taken the field. Deciding to ignore the menace of Fort Niagara to his communications, Brown crossed the Niagara River in two divisions above and below Fort Erie on the night of the 2nd of July; and in the evening of the 3rd received the bloodless surrender of the garrison of Fort Erie itself.

This, considering the small numbers of the British in the field, was a serious mishap. Either the post should not have been held at all, or its commander, Major Buck of the Eighth, should have defended it to the last; and it is clear that Buck did not do his duty. On the 4th Brown pushed General Scott's brigade twelve miles northward to Street's Creek, a small stream two miles south of the Chippewa, which was the first British line of defence, pressing back the British advanced parties before him. In rear of the Chippewa, which is fifty yards wide, General Riall—in the absence of Drummond at Kingston—had collected a force of about eleven hundred regulars and three hundred militia and Indians, and would have attacked Brown on that very day but that he was expecting the arrival of the Eighth from York.

As things were, he contented himself with pushing forward a squadron of the Nineteenth Light Dragoons and two companies of the Hundredth to reconnoitre, and was not deterred from his purpose by the intelligence that the enemy force was superior to his own. Drummond, indeed, after the experience of his last campaign, had instructed him that he might take liberties with the American infantry; nor could Riall divine that the troops before him were much superior to any that the British had yet encountered, and that they were no longer led by such feeble creatures as Hull, Dearborn, Smith and Wilkinson, but by a fighting commander.

On the morning of the 5th the Eighth came up, having made a forced march from their landing-place; and at four in the afternoon Riall crossed the Chippewa with his whole force and three guns. He then advanced southward in three columns, covered by an advanced guard, with his left on the Niagara River and his right flank shielded against attack from the forest by a flank guard of Indians and militia. As it happened, Scott at the same moment was moving northward from Street's Creek, not with any idea of fighting, but in order to drill his men in the open space between the two streams.

A thin belt of forest stretching across this cleared ground concealed the two forces from each other; and Riall's flanking party penetrating through this belt, began to, annoy the advanced parties which screened Scott's left. General Brown, who was in front reconnoitring, thereupon ordered up his Indians and militia, who thrust back Riall's regulars, but upon emerging at the further side of the belt were met by the light companies of the British regulars and militia, and driven off in hopeless rout. Brown, realising the situation, at once galloped away to fetch the remainder of his army, shouting to Scott as he passed to prepare for an engagement.

Hastily throwing a battalion into the wood to cover the retreat of the flying Indians and militia, Scott drew up the remainder of his brigade with its right to the Niagara river, while Riall continued to advance clear of the belt of wood, thus laying bare his own right flank. Scott's left flank being likewise in the air, Riall unlimbered his three pieces to play upon the enemy's right, and leaving the Eighth, apparently, to support the guns, formed the Royal Scots and Hundredth to attack the American left. Scott met this manoeuvre by filing his left wing away still further to his left, until he overlapped the two British regiments, when he deployed it and opened fire.

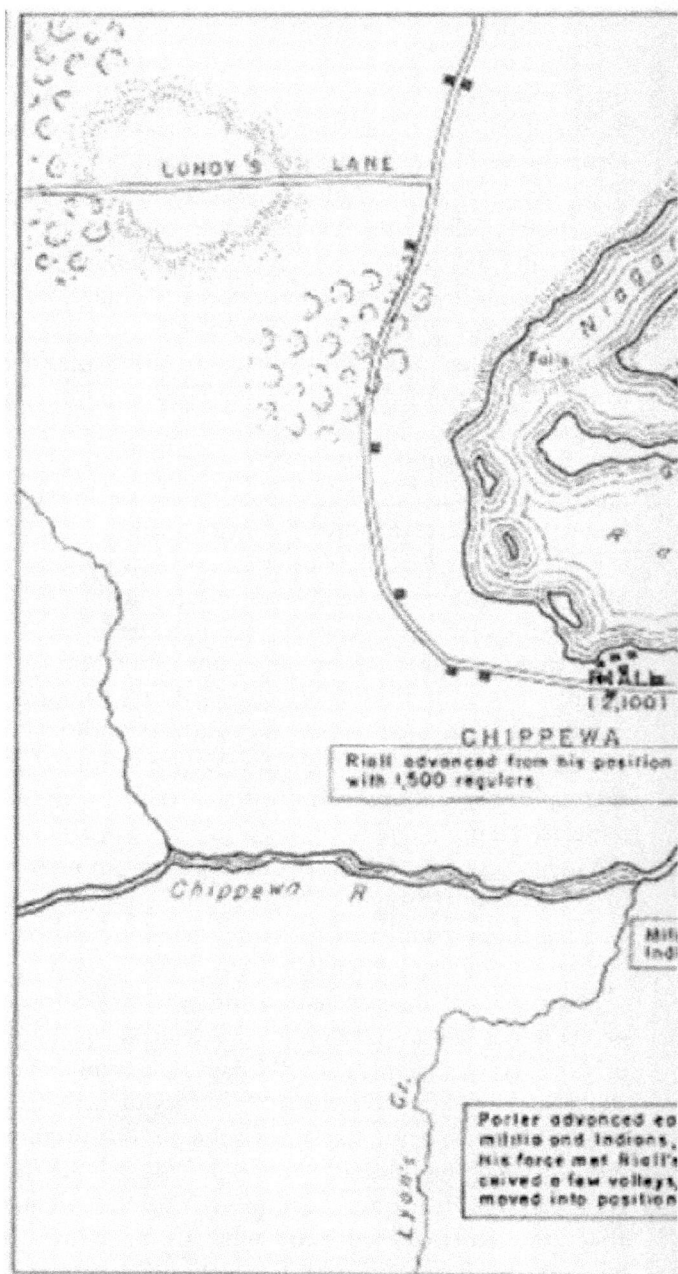

LUNDY'S LANE

Niagara

Falls

R

HALL
(2,100)

CHIPPEWA

Riall advanced from his position
with 1,500 regulars

Chippewa R

Mili
Indi

Lyon's Cr

Porter advanced ea
militia and Indians,
His force met Riall's
ceived a few volleys,
moved into position

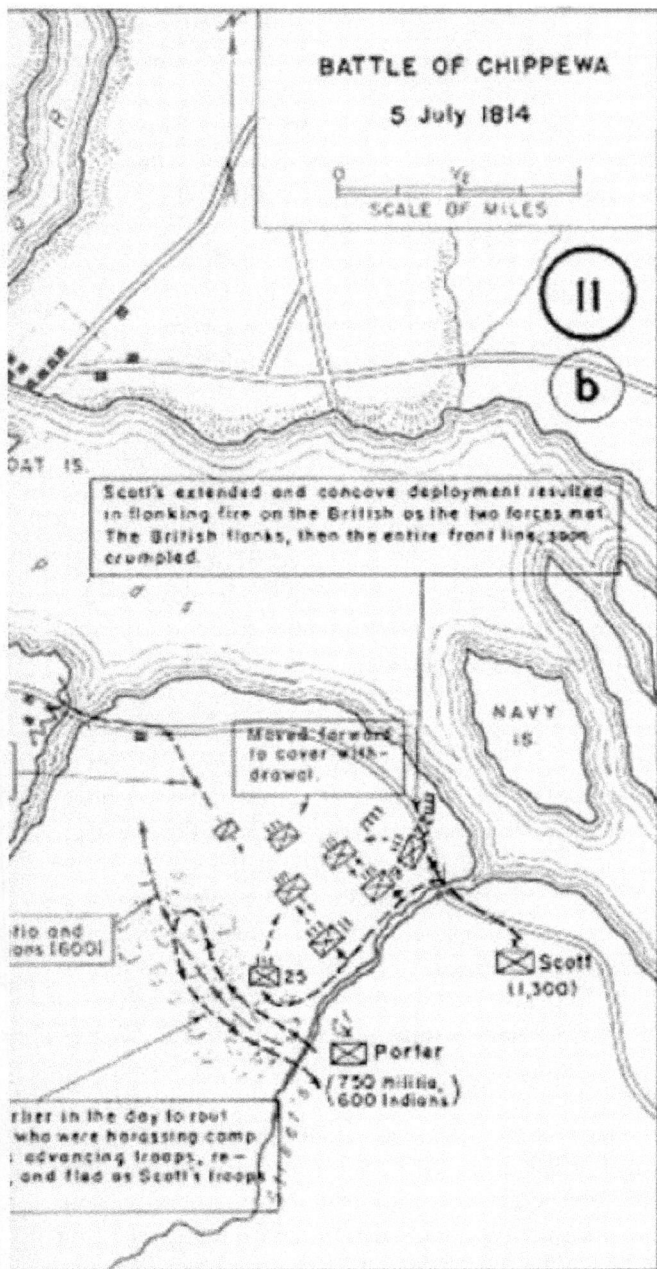

BATTLE OF CHIPPEWA
5 July 1814

SCALE OF MILES

Scott's extended and concave deployment resulted in flanking fire on the British as the two forces met. The British flanks, then the entire front line, soon crumpled.

NAVY IS.

Moved forward to cover withdrawal.

...tio and ...ns (600)

Scott (1,300)

Porter
(750 militia, 600 Indians)

...rlier in the day to rout ...who were harassing camp ...advancing troops, re- ...and fled as Scott's troops

This deployment was executed by the Americans with admirable regularity, and seems to have anticipated that of the First and Hundredth, who however met them steadily enough, though the American fire was seen to be superior. Both sides now advanced, halting from time to time to pour volleys into each other until Brown's remaining brigade was seen coming up upon Scott's left; whereupon Scott, being thus assured of support, wheeled up his left wing so as to edge his opponents closer into the fire of his right wing. Riall made a last effort to save the day by summoning the Eighth to his right, and ordering the First and Hundredth to charge; but the two gallant regiments being caught under a cross fire, suffered so severely that he was fain to call them off and to retreat, covering an orderly retirement with the Light companies and the Eighth.

The change of conditions indicated by this little action was alarming for the British. Not only were the casualties of Riall's force far in excess of the American losses—five hundred and fifteen as against three hundred and thirty-one, (British loss: 148 killed; 321 wounded; 46 missing. American loss: 56 killed; 239 wounded; 36 missing),—but in actual fact Riall had been beaten by Scott's brigade alone, which had no preponderance in numbers. (The casualties of Scott's brigade were 44 killed; 224 wounded. The casualties of Ripley's brigade were 3 killed; 3 wounded). It is true that Scott, being assured of the support of Brown's remaining brigade—that of Ripley—could throw the whole of his troops into action at once, whereas Riall was obliged to hold the Eighth in reserve, so that the British commander was justified in saying that he contended with an enemy numerically superior.

The manoeuvres in the combat, despite of the details given in the autobiography of Scott and in Riall's report, are obscure; but there is no doubt that the British troops behaved admirably, as sufficiently attested by the losses of the First and Hundredth, which amounted to close upon half of their numbers. (1/1st. 1 off., 62 men killed; 10 off., 125 men wounded; 30 men missing = 228. 100th. 2 off., 67 men killed; 9 off., 125 men wounded; I off. missing = 204. There were no unwounded prisoners).

Still the British were beaten, and it was evident that the experience of two campaigns had at last turned the Americans into soldiers who were not to be trifled with. Drummond's position therefore became most critical. At the outset his men had been none too many, and now they had been diminished by nearly seven hundred, not far from one-fifth of the entire force. Moreover, the loss of Detroit in the previous

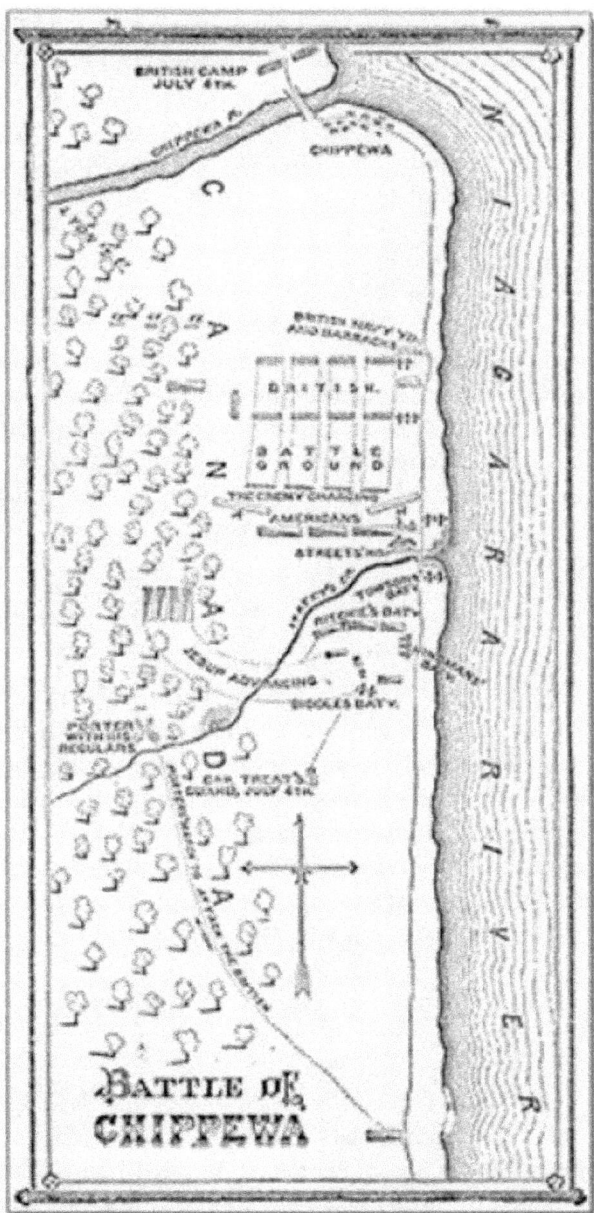

BATTLE OF
CHIPPEWA

year had left his right, or western flank, unprotected, and rendered a precarious situation doubly insecure.

After the action Riall fell back upon Chippewa, unmolested by the Americans; but Brown, following him up, turned the position and compelled the British to retire towards Burlington. On the 10th Brown reached Queenston, and there for some days he halted, eagerly awaiting the arrival of Chauncey's fleet to bring him heavy guns, cut off the British communications by water, and co-operate generally in bringing the campaign to a decisive issue. Chauncey, however, who had announced that he would sail on the 1st, gave no sign of doing so, but, to the dismay of his government no less than of Brown, found pretext after pretext for delay, and in fact did not leave Sackett's until the 1st of August.

Meanwhile Brown waited in painful suspense. On the 15th he made a reconnaissance in force, which moved round Fort George as far as Lake Ontario, but failed to entice Riall from his lines. On the 20th he moved his entire army before Fort St. George and began to throw up siege-works; whereupon Riall, seriously alarmed, sent pressing requests for reinforcements to Drummond at York, but still refrained, though with an effort, from coming out to fight. After waiting for two days Brown on the 22nd retired to Queenston, and Riall advanced with seventeen hundred regular troops and about a thousand militia and Indians to Twenty Mile Creek.

On the 23rd Brown learned definitely that it was hopeless to look for Chauncey's arrival; and on the 25th he fell back to Chippewa, designing to march rapidly thence upon Burlington Heights and York. Thus matters stood at a deadlock; and the only important incident at this time was the wanton burning of the villages of Queenston and St. David's by the American militia. Brown, to his honour, dismissed the officer who had ordered the destruction of St. David's; but the mischief had been done and was destined to produce serious consequences.

On the 22nd Drummond returned from Kingston to York, bringing with him four hundred of the Eighty-Ninth and the flank companies of the Hundred and Fourth, which had been relieved by the arrival of the Sixth, Eighty-Second, Nova Scotia Fencibles and one wing of the First (4th batt., lately on service with Graham at Bergen-op-Zoom; Prevost to Sec. of State, 12th July 1814), in the St. Lawrence two days earlier. Without delay he planned an offensive stroke against Brown's communications from Fort Niagara, and with that object sent

PLAN OF THE
BATTLE
OF
LUNDY'S LANE
10 O'CLOCK

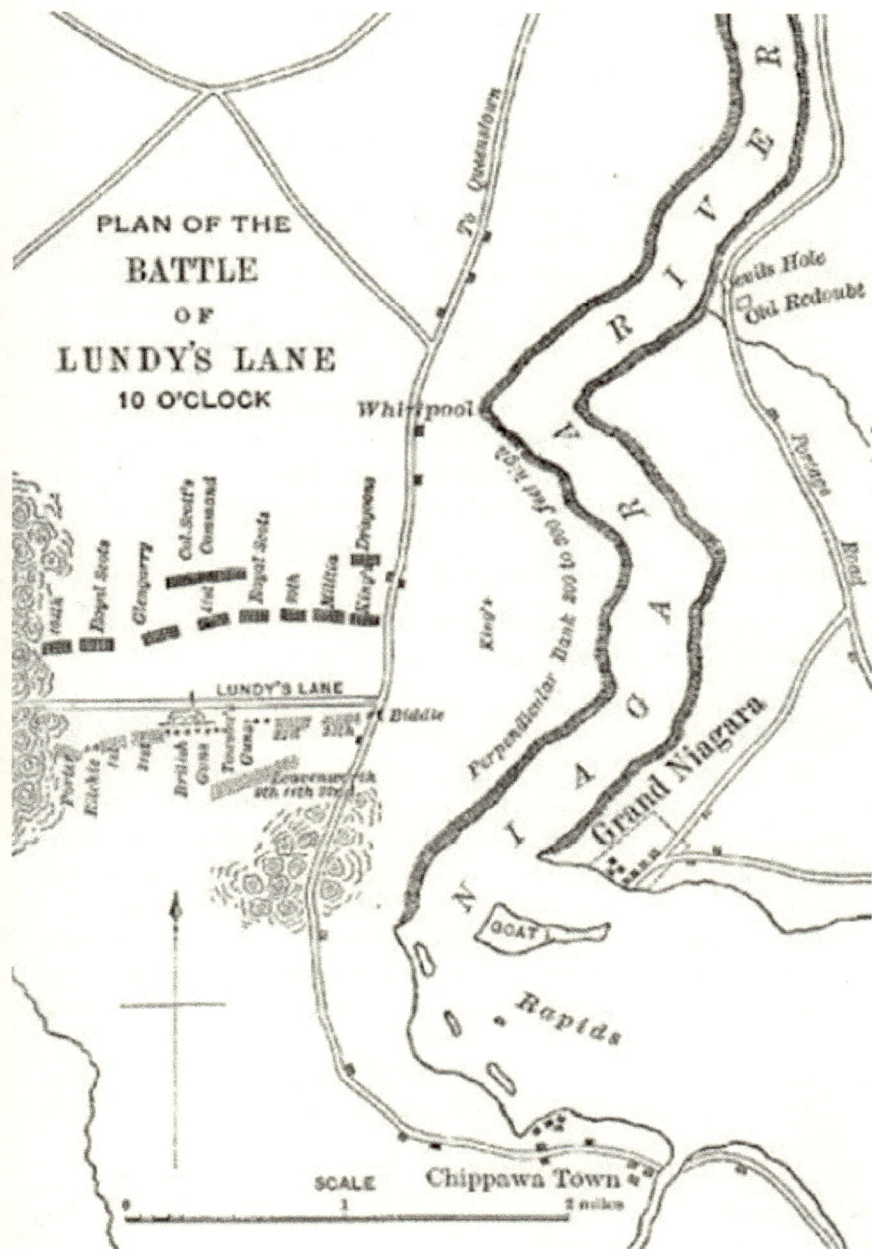

To Queenstown

Whirlpool

Devils Hole
Old Redoubt

Portage Road

R I V E R

N I A G A R A

King's

Perpendicular Bank 200 to 300 feet high

Royal Scots
Glengarry
Col. Scott's Command
41st
Royal Scots
8th
Militia
King's Dragoons
89th

LUNDY'S LANE

British Guns
Towsen's Camp
Pickets
Riflemen
Riflemen
Ricketts
Biddle

Leavenworth
9th 11th 22nd

Grand Niagara

GOAT I.

Rapids

SCALE
0   1   2 miles

Chippawa Town

the Eighty-Ninth and his flank companies to that fort on the 23rd; ordering the commandant, Colonel Tucker, to strengthen himself further by drawing men from the posts on the other side of the river, and to move with some fifteen hundred men upon Brown's advanced base at Lewiston.

The operation was appointed to take place at daylight of the 25th; and Riall was directed simultaneously to advance against Brown, but to decline a general action unless it were forced upon him by the enemy, in which case Tucker was to cross the water to his assistance. At dawn of the 25th Drummond himself arrived at Fort Niagara, when, ascertaining that Riall had already made a forward movement, he modified his orders; transferring the Eighty-Ninth and some of the detachments to the command of Colonel Morrison with instructions to move through Queenston to the support of Riall, and leaving Tucker only some five hundred soldiers, together with some seamen and Indians, for the march upon Lewiston. The seamen were taken from four small vessels which, looking to Chauncey's inactivity, Yeo had ventured to spare to carry troops, supplies and stores to Niagara. Drummond wrote some days later:

Without their help I should certainly not have been able to attempt offensive operations so soon after my arrival.

These changes caused some delay in the march of Tucker, who upon reaching Lewiston at noon found that the Americans had already retreated, carrying with them their guns, but abandoning tents, stores and provisions, which fell into the hands of the British. Tucker then ferried his troops across from Lewiston to Queenston, where they joined hands with Morrison's, which had awaited them at that point. After a halt, most of the Forty-First and Hundredth regiments were sent back to the forts, and Drummond with the Eighty-Ninth, the light company of the Forty-First and detachments of the First and Eighth—some nine hundred of all ranks—at about four o'clock continued his march.

Riall had, meanwhile, at midnight of the 24th-25th pushed forward an advanced guard of about a thousand men under Lieutenant-Colonel Pearson, and these at seven o'clock occupied a hill by Lundy's Lane, about a mile to northwest of the Niagara Falls. The rest of Riall's force waited under arms at Twelve Mile creek, some eight miles to westward, until noon, when some fifteen hundred men with four guns were ordered to join Pearson. The whole of these movements on the

116

BATTLE OF LUNDY'S LANE

BATTLE OF LUNDY'S LANE

Situation About 6:00 P.M., 25 July 1814

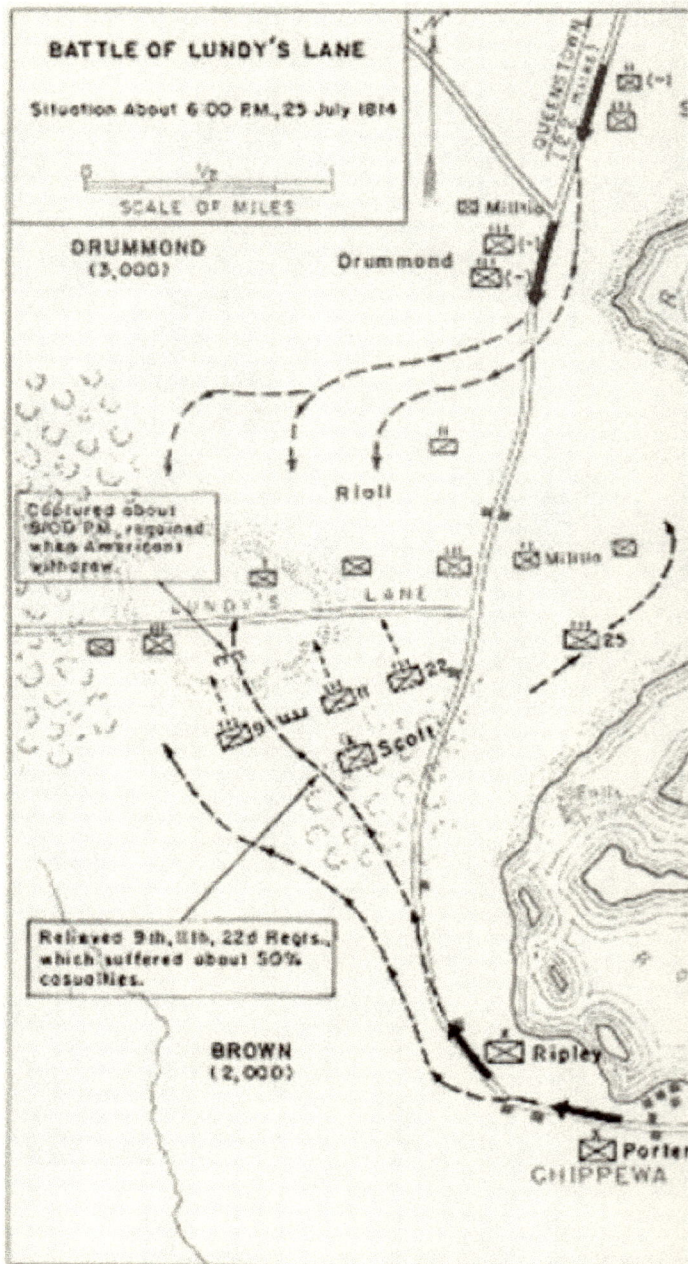

SCALE OF MILES

DRUMMOND
(3,000)

Drummond

Militia

Riall

Captured about
6:00 P.M., regained
when Americans
withdrew.

LUNDY'S LANE

Militia

25

22

Scott

9

11

Relieved 9th, 11th, 22d Regts.,
which suffered about 50%
casualties.

BROWN
(2,000)

Ripley

Porter

CHIPPEWA

C

Scott

DEVIL'S HOLE

OLD REDOUBT

NOTE: Scott attempted a frontal attack by the 9th, 11th,
and 22d Regts. and an envelopment by the 25th.
The 25th succeeded in gaining the rear of the line
but was later forced to withdraw. The frontal attack,
pressed persistently against a strong position and
heavy arty. fire, failed with severe losses. Simultaneously at dark the reinforcements of both sides
arrived, and the battle seesawed across the ridge
until midnight, when both sides withdrew. Neither
side held out a reserve, so that at critical stages,
when a fresh regiment might have decided the
battle, none was available.

NIAGARA

GOAT IS

NAVY
IS.

Canadian side were unknown to Brown, who, however, was informed, apparently rather late, of Tucker's raid upon Lewiston; when fearing that it might be extended to a more important American depot at Fort Schlosser, he decided to make a diversion by advancing upon Queenston.

At a little before five accordingly General Scott's brigade came upon Pearson's detachment, the strength of which had evidently been underestimated by the American scouts; for Scott hesitated to attack, and despatched a message to Brown for reinforcements. Riall, on his side, mistaking Scott's brigade for Brown's whole force, ordered his main body from Twelve Mile Creek, which was still three miles distant, to take up a position on Queenston heights, and himself directed the retreat of Pearson's detachment to that point. On the way he met Drummond, who took personal command of Pearson's troops and turned them back to reoccupy Lundy's Lane, sending word to the main body from Twelve Mile Creek to hasten with all speed to the same point.

The position of Lundy's Lane consisted of a low hill, about a mile in length from east to west by less than half a mile in depth from north to south, which rises to a height of about twenty-five feet above a long gradual slope. It was traversed from east to west by the road known as Lundy's Lane, and was bounded on each flank by two more roads which ran parallel to each other from north to south, the more easterly being the road to Queenston. The southern and eastern slopes were covered with wood, and on the side of the river were skirted by swamps also, which gave some imperfect protection to the eastern flank; but, weak though the position was, it was the only one south of Queenston Heights that offered an advantage for resisting a hostile advance from the south. Had General Scott pushed his force boldly forward he might easily have secured the hill; but dreading an ambush he had felt his way cautiously towards it, and was still six hundred yards distant, when Drummond with some seventeen hundred men crossed the summit.

Unlimbering two five-pounders upon the highest point, Drummond formed his line in rear of them and on the reverse slope of the hill; the Glengarry regiment on the extreme right bestriding the cross-roads on the western side, with a part or the whole of the Royal Scots, Forty-First, Eighty-Ninth and Eighth in succession upon the left of the Glengarry. The left flank of the Eighth rested on the Queenston road, with a battalion of militia beyond it; and one troop of the Nineteenth Light Dragoons stood on the road to their left rear.

The array was slightly concave in form, and had hardly been completed when at half-past six Scott came up with his own brigade only, and, making a demonstration along the whole front, detached a column through the woods against Drummond's left flank. After the lapse of an hour this detachment fell upon the militia battalion, which formed the extreme left of Drummond's line, and drove it back, together with the little party of the Nineteenth Light Dragoons, in some confusion. Several prisoners were taken; and General Riall, who was wounded at this juncture, being carried in the wrong direction owing to the growing darkness, fell into the hands of the enemy.

The militia quickly rallied, however, forming *en potence* along the Queenston road, and effectually secured Drummond's left flank from further danger. Meanwhile the first of Brown's reinforcements came up, and were thrown by Scott against the British centre; but the attack was repulsed after severe fighting with heavy loss, and Drummond remained in possession of the hill.

It was now between eight and nine o'clock, and there was a lull in the action except for a duel of artillery, while both generals busied themselves in re-forming their array for a fresh combat. By this time the whole of Brown's army had arrived, and the detachment from Twelve Mile Creek had at last joined Drummond, much harassed and fatigued by a long day of marches and counter-marches. The British general, fearing for his right flank, extended his line on that side by placing the seven companies of the Royal Scots on the right of the Glengarries, and the flank companies of the Hundred and Fourth on the right of the Royal Scots. He formed the remainder in second line, a few companies of the Eighth in the centre, with some militia on their right, and the Hundred and Third, which was a young regiment, on their left. Brown on his side drew up two battalions in dead ground at the foot of the hill, and directed them to storm the British battery, which had now been increased by a third gun. The Americans rushed forward gallantly enough.

The battalion which advanced over the open was repulsed with heavy loss; but the other crept up through the woods to a log-fence within twenty yards of the British cannon, poured in a volley, charged, bayoneted the gunners while in the act of loading, and then turned the pieces against the British line. More infantry followed them, and the American artillery likewise ascended the hill at a gallop. One gun, having lost all its drivers by a volley, was carried by the horses into the

Enemy reconnoitering

Scott's
Brigade

⚔ Town
⚔ Batt

Enemy's Advance

Chippawa Road
Mrs Wilson's

Niagara
Falls

Goat I.

NIAGARA

BATTLE OF LUNDY'S LANE
JULY 25th 1814

Glen

104th

Lundy's Lane

89th
Detachments
Royal Scots
41st

Church

Queenston Road

Jessup's
Movement

Militia

19th
Light
Dragoons

Detachment
8th Regt

British Reserves
Advancing

RIVER →

ranks of the British and was secured; but this for a time was the only success upon Drummond's side.

Bringing up his four remaining guns, he endeavoured to restore the fight; and these and the American pieces fired almost muzzle to muzzle. They were taken and retaken, and the combat resolved itself into a savage struggle between small units and individuals for the summit of the hill. All order was lost in the darkness; battalions, companies and even sections became intermixed, and the fight was carried on with the bayonet, with the butt, with any weapon that came to hand. Brown and Scott were both of them wounded and disabled. Drummond also was severely hurt, but continued in command.

For three long hours the battle continued, the Americans, apparently, retaining the summit of the hill, but unable to carry off the British guns or to improve their advantage under the incessant fire of their enemies. At last, just before midnight, Brown ordered General Ripley to draw off his troops and retreat to Chippewa, and at dawn the British reoccupied the crest and recovered their guns. Superior discipline had told, and the victory—such as it was—rested with them.

This was the best contested fight of the whole war. If we are to accept American figures, (Mahan, ii.), the numbers engaged were nearly equal—about twenty-eight hundred of all ranks on each side—with a slight preponderance of regular troops in favour of the Americans, and a superiority of seven guns against two in favour of the British. The casualties of the British numbered eight hundred and seventy-eight, of whom eighty-four were killed. (British loss: 84 killed; 559 wounded; 193 missing; 42 prisoners. American loss: 171 killed; 572 wounded; 117 missing).

Those of the Americans, according to their official report, did not exceed eight hundred and sixty, of whom one hundred and seventy-one were killed. In the matter of the numbers actually killed and wounded the Americans by their own showing exceeded the British by nearly one hundred; but, whereas Drummond reported the capture of several hundreds of prisoners, the American return of missing shows no more than one hundred and seventeen. Drummond may certainly have been guilty of exaggeration; but on the whole I distrust the American figures, both as to casualties and as to their strength on the field; and I incline to the belief that they had certainly four thousand men present, and that they lost a thousand of them. Trophies were almost evenly divided, the Americans carrying off one British gun, which they mistook for one of their own, and leaving two of their own behind them.

The brunt of the action fell upon the Eighty-Ninth, which went into action about four hundred strong and lost two hundred and seventeen killed and wounded, and upon the Royal Scots, who added one hundred and thirty hurt and slain to the two hundred and seventy who had already fallen at Chippewa. Altogether it was a stout little fight, honourable alike to Americans and British. (American writers are fond of asserting that some of the Peninsular veterans were present at Lundy's Lane, this is, of course, untrue).

On the following day General Ripley advanced by Brown's order to bring off his dead, wounded and artillery. Finding the British in occupation of the field he immediately retired, broke down the bridge over the river, threw the greatest part of his baggage, supplies and stores into the rapids, and retreated with much haste and not in the best order to Fort Erie. Drummond's light troops and Indians followed him and made a few prisoners; and Ripley busied himself in enlarging and strengthening the defences of the fort in anticipation of an attack.

Drummond, after repairing the bridge and receiving reinforcements which raised his numbers to over three thousand men, likewise advanced, and on the 3rd of August invested Fort Erie. The place was formidable with new earthworks and batteries, extending from the fort to the edge of the lake, and flanked on the side of the river by the guns of Black Rock, and on the side of the lake by three gun-boats. On the night of the 3rd Drummond made an unsuccessful attempt to surprise Black Rock; and two days later the besieged were heartened by the arrival of General Gaines to supersede Ripley in chief command.

On the same day a more formidable enemy arrived in the shape of Commodore Chauncey with his squadron, who promptly intercepted and drove ashore a British brig, and, leaving three of his vessels to watch for British small craft in the Niagara River, sailed back to the blockade of Kingston. This was discouraging, for Drummond had already broken ground and begun to raise a battery before Fort Erie; but without naval command of Lake Ontario he was likely to run short of ammunition. On the night of the 12th Captain Dobbs of the Royal Navy attacked the three vessels on Lake Erie in open boats, capturing two of them and chasing away the third; and Drummond, having opened fire on the 13th, gave orders for the delivery of the assault before dawn of the 15th.

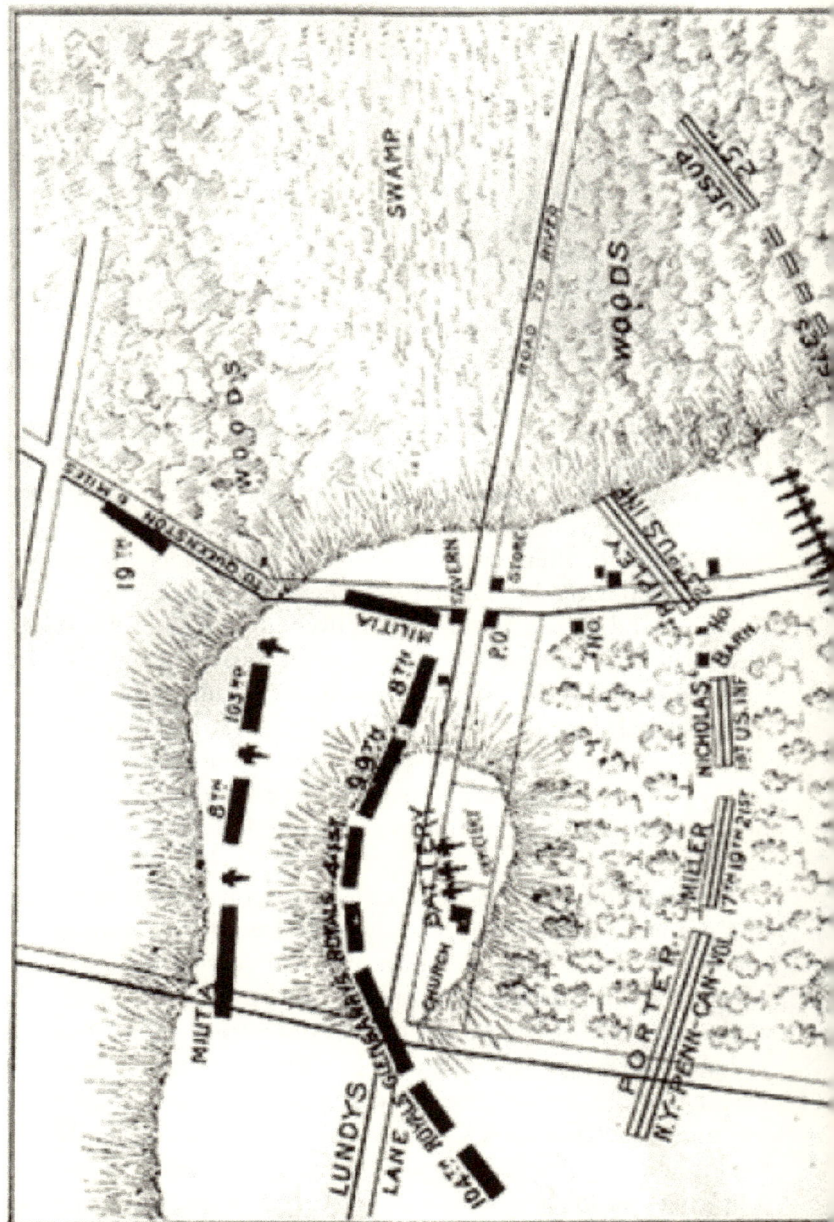

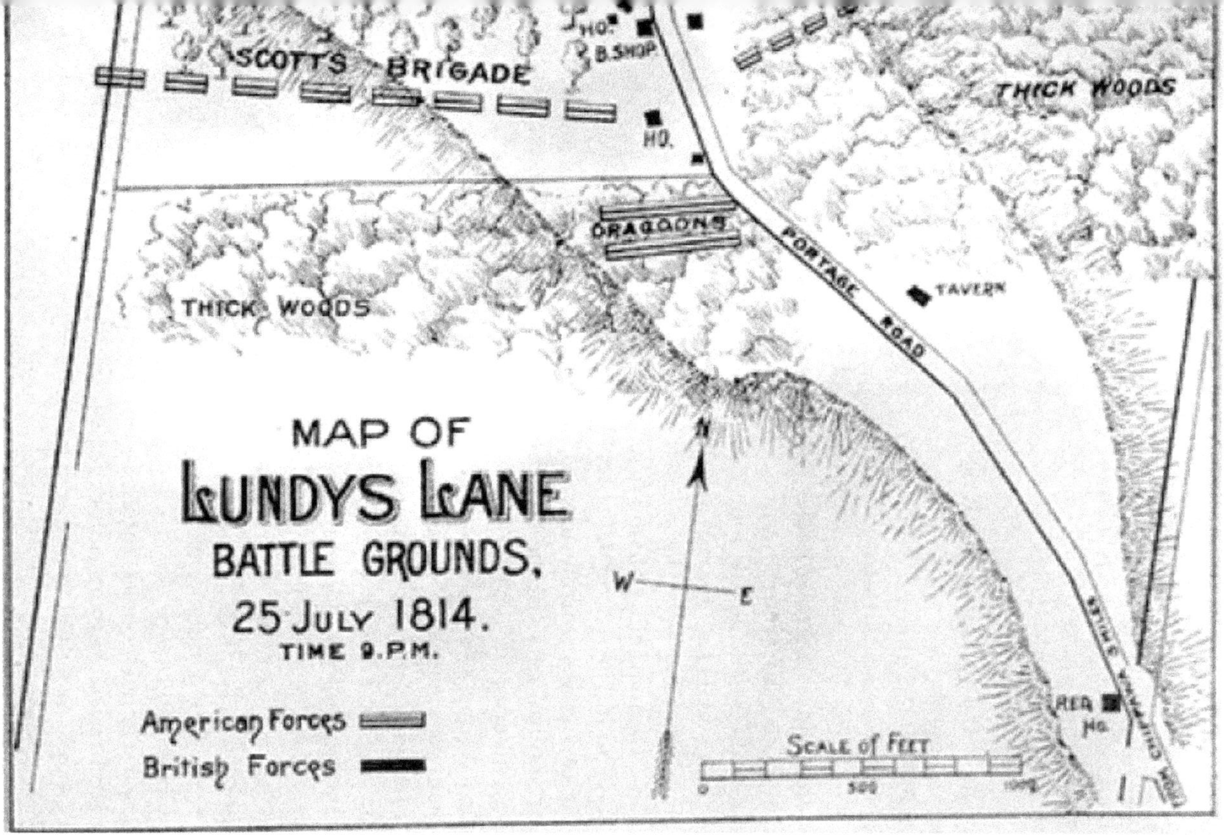

MAP OF
LUNDYS LANE
BATTLE GROUNDS,
25 JULY 1814.
TIME 9. P.M.

American Forces
British Forces

SCALE OF FEET

THICK WOODS

PORTAGE ROAD

TAVERN

DRAGOONS

SCOTT'S BRIGADE

THICK WOODS

B. SHOP

HO.

HO.

HEAD
QUARTERS

FROM CHIPPEWA 2 MILES

N

W

E

Fort Erie, as constructed by the British, stood about an hundred yards from the shore, where the Niagara River flows out of Lake Erie. The Americans had extended the defences eastward by earthworks to the strand, erecting a stone fort named the Douglas battery at the water's edge, and southward also by half a mile of earthworks to a sandy knoll called Snake Hill, from which point the shore of the lake begins to turn westward. This knoll likewise was crowned by a battery, and connected with the water by a line of palisades. The whole of this enclosure was covered by ditches and abatis, and was garrisoned—though of this Drummond was not aware—by a force exceeding his own in numbers.

General Drummond decided to attack in three columns. The strongest of these, thirteen hundred in numbers, under Colonel Fischer of Watteville's, was to assail Snake Hill; the second, about two hundred and fifty strong, under Lieutenant-Colonel Drummond of the Hundred and Fourth, was to carry the old fort; and the third, of about six hundred and fifty men, under Colonel Hercules Scott of the Hundred and Third, was to fall upon the Douglas battery. (Fischer's column: Watteville's, 8th; light cos. 89th and 100th; a few cavalry and artillery. Drummond's column: flank cos. 41st and 104th; dets. bluejackets and marines. Scott's column: 2 cos. Royal Scots; 103rd).

At two o'clock in the morning the attack was opened by Fischer, who had removed the flints from his men's muskets in order to ensure silence and surprise. A few men of the two flank companies turned the line of palisades by wading through the lake; but the mass of them were checked by the abatis, and, giving way under a storm of shot from the American muskets and rifles, threw the supports, which in the darkness had entangled themselves in difficult ground by the water, into hopeless confusion. Watteville's regiment broke, carrying away with it in its flight nearly all the remainder of the column; and the small parties which had entered the lines, being unsustained, were compelled to fall back.

At the sound of the cannonade the two remaining columns moved forward to their work. That of Scott was driven back with heavy loss by the fire of the Douglas battery, and joined that of Lieutenant-Colonel Drummond in the assault of the old fort. This last attacked with the greatest resolution, and after three repulses succeeded in establishing themselves in one of the bastions, from which they turned the guns upon the Douglas battery. The Americans strove desperately to dislodge them, but in vain. All seemed to be in good train, when a store of ammunition which had been accumulated in the bastion was accidentally, as it seems, exploded, and blew the bastion and the whole of its occupants into the air. Panic followed instantaneously. The survivors of the column ran back in disorder, and General Drummond was fain to throw out the Royal Scots for the protection of their retreat, and to abandon the entire enterprise.

The British casualties amounted to nine hundred and five, over five hundred men being returned as missing, who were probably killed or wounded by the explosion. The heaviest of the loss fell upon the Hundred and Third, which, with nearly one hundred and forty wounded and over two hundred and eighty missing, was practically annihilated, and upon the flank companies of the Forty-First, whose casualties exceeded eighty. Watteville's also suffered severely, nearly one hundred and fifty officers and men having fallen; but this regiment was considered, justly or unjustly, to have behaved ill. Drummond wrote, in a sentence which was omitted from the despatch printed in the *Gazette*:

> Had the troops of Fischer's column been steady only for a few minutes the enemy must have fled from his works and have surrendered.

A corps composed of mercenaries of all nations, Poles, Germans, Dutch and Portuguese, was not likely to have the same cohesion as a British battalion; but no troops in the world are exempt from the peril of panic, especially when their own fugitive comrades crash into them in the darkness. Drummond was certainly unlucky, for his men actually penetrated the American works at two different points, and might well have held their own at the old fort but for the accident of the explosion. But these are mere commonplaces of the fortune of war. Night attacks upon fortified positions are in the last degree hazardous and uncertain, and this particular night attack was a disastrous failure. The Americans stated their loss to be one hundred and twenty-eight, and, whether this figure be correct or not, their casualties cannot in any case have exceeded one-fourth of the British. Gaines and his troops had every reason to plume themselves upon their success.

Reduced to impotence through the weakening of his force and the interruption of his communications by water, Drummond was practically obliged to turn the siege into a blockade. The first reinforcements from the Peninsular Army—the Sixth and Eighty-Second—had arrived in the St. Lawrence early in July, (Prevost to Sec. of State, 12th July 1814); but, though forwarded up country with all

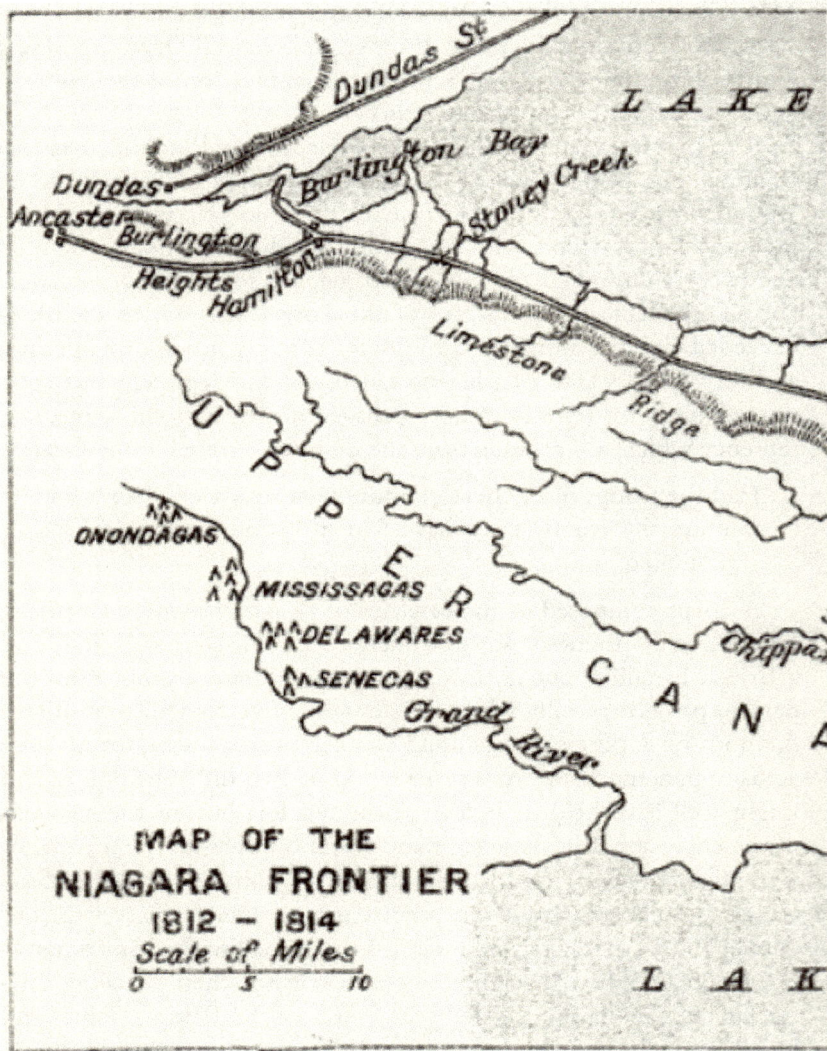

Dundas St.

Dundas

Ancaster
Burlington
Heights
Hamilton

Burlington Bay

Stoney Creek

LAKE

Limestone

Ridge

U
P
P
E
R

ONONDAGAS

MISSISSAGAS

DELAWARES

SENECAS

Grand River

C
A
N
A

Chippa

MAP OF THE
NIAGARA FRONTIER
1812 — 1814
Scale of Miles
0   5   10

LAKE

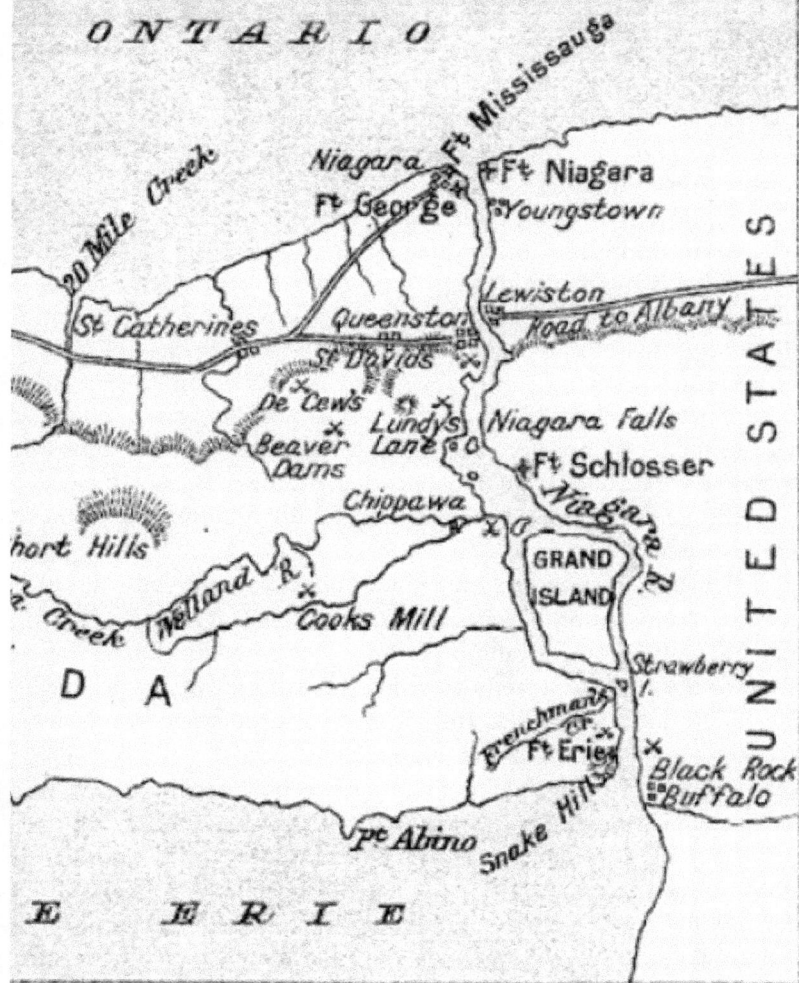

possible speed, the Eighty-second, owing to the wretched state of the roads, did not reach Drummond until the 29th of August, nor the Sixth until the 2nd of September. Supplies and stores, however, could only be brought by water, and, though Drummond continued the construction of batteries within closer range of the American works, he was short of ammunition and very anxious about victuals. From the first week of September the blockade of Kingston became rigorous; and even the passage from York to Niagara was so unsafe that Drummond dared not call up further reinforcements lest he should be unable to feed them.

Commodore Yeo, for his part, refused to move until the great ship which was to assure him of naval superiority should be completed; and his policy is perfectly intelligible. But naval superiority was, after all, only a means to an end; and there was always the danger lest, while the means were preparing, the end might be sacrificed. To add to Drummond's difficulties the season was wet and unhealthy; and unceasing sickness among the troops from this cause and from want of provisions inclined him more and more to raise the siege and retreat to Chippewa. His resolution was hastened by the action of Brown, who at the beginning of September had resumed command of the American Army.

The British batteries were three in number, situated in the midst of thickets, about five hundred yards distant from the American lines and a mile and a half from Drummond's main encampment. On the afternoon of the 17th of September, when the batteries were in charge of the Eighth and Watteville's, Brown made a sortie with two thousand men, sending one column under General Porter through the woods round the British right and rear, and keeping a second column under General Miller hidden in a ravine before the British centre. The movement was exceedingly well executed. Porter managed to approach unperceived very near the British right-hand battery; and, Miller simultaneously penetrating the line of picquets between it and the centre battery, the two columns converged upon the right-hand battery and mastered it in a few minutes.

After destroying the guns, the two commanders proceeded against the centre battery, which, after a sharp resistance, was also captured. Before serious damage could be done to the guns, however, Drummond's reserves came up; and the Royal Scots, Sixth, Eighty-Second and Eighty-Ninth, with the Glengarries, speedily swept the enemy out of the captured works and back to their entrenchments, with the loss of rather over five hundred killed, wounded and prisoners. The casualties of the British in this counter-attack barely exceeded two hundred, showing that the Americans were still unable to meet veteran troops in the field; but of the Eighth and Watteville's two hundred and fifty were taken prisoners, besides over one hundred slain or hurt, which raised the British loss to a total of six hundred and nine. Since three British guns also had been destroyed the balance of advantage in this affair lay decidedly with the Americans.

Four days later Drummond, though he had lately been strengthened by the arrival of the Ninety-Seventh, broke up his camp and retreated to Chippewa. Thirteen days of incessant rain had not only swelled his sick list alarmingly, but had undermined the foundations of Fort Niagara and Fort George. Reinforcements could reach the army only by driblets; and the difficulties of insecure communication harassed him perpetually. On the 24th he fixed his headquarters at the falls of Niagara, cantoning his troops along the line of the river from Black Creek to Lake Ontario, with Chippewa for the point of concentration. Brown made no attempt to follow him, mistrusting his own weakness; and the two forces remained supine, until on the 5th of October General Izard with his army arrived at Lewiston from Lake Champlain. His coming was due to the confused strategical notions of Secretary Armstrong.

At the end of July this gentleman had suggested that Izard should advance against either Montreal or Prescott, as a diversion to save Brown in case larger reinforcements should be sent to Drummond. The news of Brown's retreat, however, altered the situation; and on the 12th of August Armstrong suggested that Izard should march to Sackett's Harbour, and embark two thousand men there for Fort Erie.

It is difficult to see the object of this movement. Brown was in no danger—he had in fact represented Lundy's Lane to be a victory—for the Americans held the command of the water on Lake Ontario; and, so long as they did so, Drummond's situation was precarious. On the other hand on Lake Champlain there was much to be feared, for British infantry from France had been pouring into the St. Lawrence during the first part of August, and was not likely to remain idle.

However, Izard meekly obeyed, marched four thousand men to Sackett's Harbour, embarked twenty-five hundred of them there on the 21st of September, landed these at the Genesee on the south shore of Lake Ontario on the 22nd, and on the 27th met Brown in consultation at Batavia. As the result of this conference Izard, who was the senior officer, decided to besiege Fort Niagara, and to that end marched for Lewiston; but at a second council of war it was determined to concentrate on the American side of the Niagara River south of the Chippewa, and to undertake no sieges until Drummond's force had been accounted for.

On the 10th and 11th of October Izard passed his army over the Niagara near Black Rock; and, encamping two miles from Fort Erie, marched down stream on the 13th upon Drummond's lines at Chippewa. Drummond watched him with perfect equanimity, for the British front was unassailable, their left flank covered by the Niagara, and the country on their right impassable except by infantry, to meet which he had a superior force of artillery. Izard came up before the British position on the 15th, reconnoitred it in force, and, disliking the appearance of it, retired again to Fort Erie in abject helplessness.

On the next day he heard that Chauncey had withdrawn his fleet to Sackett's Harbour and was throwing up defensive works, that officer being unwilling to wait for the coming of Yeo's new ship, the *St. Lawrence*, which on the 14th of October was at last fit for commission. Izard, conscious that much would be expected of him with a force of six thousand fairly trained troops, wrote querulously to Armstrong bemoaning his hard fate in wanting an enterprise upon which to employ them. It never occurred to him at any time to leave Brown to contain Drummond at Chippewa and, transferring his own force to Lake Erie, to threaten the British rear from Grand River or Long Point.

On the 21st of October he broke up his camp, sent Brown with his troops to Sackett's Harbour, and began to transfer his own force to the American shore. On the 5th of November he blew up Fort Erie, and withdrew altogether from British territory. Four days earlier, by a curious irony, Yeo had sailed for Niagara with supplies, stores and a reinforcement of twelve hundred men, (37th; dets. of 6th and 82nd; 1 co. R.A. Prevost to Sec. of State, 1st Nov. 1814), all of which arrived too late.

So ended the campaign of 1814 in the west. There had been other petty operations on the remoter lakes in the course of the year. After sundry misfortunes to the British ships on Lake Erie in the earlier months of 1814, the naval situation had been restored and even improved by the valour and audacity of Lieutenant Worsley of the Royal Navy; and Lieutenant-Colonel Macdonall had successfully routed an expedition which had ascended the Mississippi against Mackinaw.

Late in October a party of seven hundred marauding Kentuck-

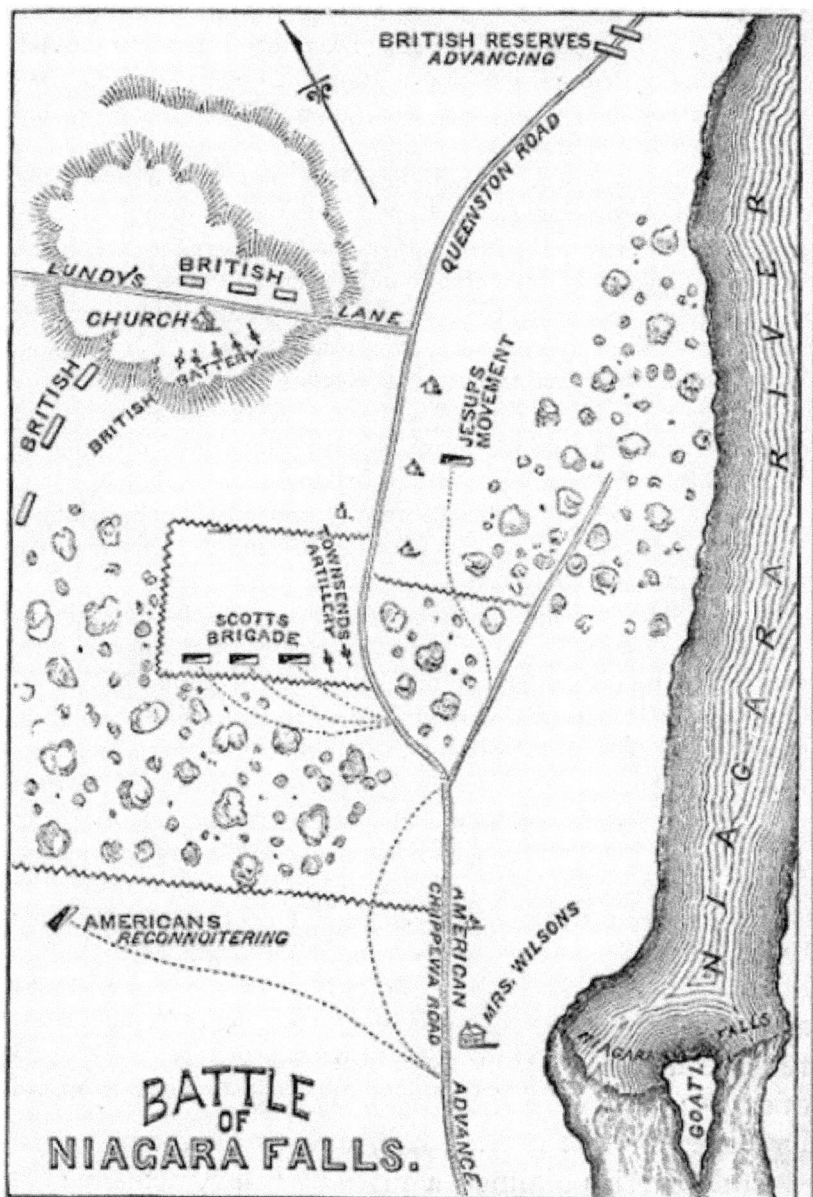

BRITISH RESERVES
ADVANCING

QUEENSTON ROAD

LUNDY'S
BRITISH
CHURCH
BATTERY
BRITISH
BRITISH
LANE

JESUPS
MOVEMENT

TOWNSENDS
ARTILLERY
SCOTTS
BRIGADE

N I A G A R A   R I V E R

AMERICANS
RECONNOITERING

AMERICAN CHIPPEWA ROAD

MRS. WILSONS

AMERICAN ADVANCE

NIAGARA FALLS

GOAT I.

BATTLE
OF
NIAGARA FALLS.

ians started from Detroit with the idea of destroying the Canadian resources in that neighbourhood, and if possible of penetrating to the head of Lake Ontario at Burlingham Heights. They were, however, turned back, before they had traversed more than half of the ground, by a menace of British troops, and accomplished no more than a considerable amount of pillage and devastation, which probably suited them better than fighting.

But all these incidents, though they ended almost invariably in the discomfiture of the Americans, were only by-issues of little importance to the contest in the peninsula of Niagara. There the Americans, though the quality of their troops and leaders had greatly improved and the improvement had been marked by two indubitable successes, had failed for the third consecutive campaign to accomplish anything. This in itself was discreditable; but far worse was the fact that the supreme director of operations in Washington had allowed himself to be distracted by a petty reverse on the western frontier into the removal of troops from the vital point, within striking distance alike of Montreal and Kingston, to the eastern head of Lake Erie. Such a blunder deserved punishment at the hands of Prevost; and we must now see what attempt he made to take advantage of the situation.

By the end of August Sir George had not far short of sixteen thousand British soldiers in Lower Canada, seven battalions of which, numbering about six thousand men, had come straight from Wellington's army in France, (these over and above the 6th and 82nd already mentioned, were 1/3rd, 1/5th, 1/9th, 3/27th, 1/39th, 57th, 1/58th).

In writing to announce the despatch of these troops Lord Bathurst informed Prevost that yet more battalions were assembling for direct attack on the American coast, and that, while not recommending any hazardous forward movement, the Cabinet hoped to see him take the offensive before the close of the campaign. The objects commended to his notice were two: first, protection, which signified the entire destruction of Sackett's Harbour and of the enemy's naval establishments on Lakes Erie and Champlain; and, secondly, permanent security, which was explained to mean the maintenance of Fort Niagara and of sufficient adjacent territory, and the occupation of Detroit and the Michigan country.

★★★★★★

Bathurst to Prevost, 3rd June 1814. Captain Mahan and Mr. Lucas both say that they have been unable to find this despatch. It is in the Record Office with the rest of the Secretary of State's despatches. C.O. 43, vol. 23.

******

This letter reached Prevost before the 14th July, enabling him to send Watteville's regiment at once to Drummond; and, as the transports began to enter the St. Lawrence at the beginning of August, he contemplated opening his campaign for the destruction of Sackett's and the occupation of Plattsburg in conjunction with the fleets on Lakes Ontario and Champlain on the 15th of September.

As regards Lake Champlain he purposed particularly to avoid any offensive movement on the eastern shore, because the State of Vermont was strongly opposed to the war, and had furnished large supplies both of specie and cattle to the British Army. Two-thirds of the troops in Canada were in fact fed on beef provided by American contractors and drawn chiefly from Vermont and New York. (Prevost to Sec. of State, 27th Aug. 1814).

Meanwhile, as the battalions arrived from the Garonne, Prevost encamped them between the Richelieu and the St. Lawrence; and by the 25th of August three brigades, under the supreme command of General de Rottenburg, were stationed along this line. (See list following)

Cavalry, 19th L.D.

Power's Brigade: 1/3rd, 1/5th, 2/27th, 1/58th.

Robinson's, Brisbane's and Kempt's Brigades: 2/8th, 19th, 13th, 3/27th, 39th, 49th, 76th, 88th; De Meuron's Canadian Chasseurs.

But Prevost had already realised that Yeo's squadron would not be ready to dominate Lake Ontario until October, or practically until three weeks later than he had expected. The first duty of the squadron must needs be to carry reinforcements and supplies of all kinds to Drummond, which would mean that offensive operations against Sackett's Harbour must be delayed for yet another week. By that time the campaigning season would be so near its end that the propriety of even beginning such operations at all would be highly questionable.

In the circumstances Sir George judged it best to send Sir James Kempt, who had arrived from France, with one brigade to Kingston, to be ready to take command of the attack upon Sackett's, and in the meanwhile to devote his own attention to Lake Champlain.

The Americans had still naval superiority upon this lake; but on the 25th of August a new British vessel, the *Confiance*, had been launched at Isle aux Noix, which was designed to be more powerful than the

137

three redoubts with blockhouses and connecting field-works held by raw levies would hardly have stopped veterans, who had carried the entrenchments of the Nivelle. The American flotilla was, it is true, anchored within range of the shore, ready to enfilade the attacking columns with its cannon; but the country, being wooded and intricate, would probably have masked the fire to a great extent; and, if Prevost were prepared in the first instance to ignore the ships, the reasonable inference is that their intervention was not greatly to be feared.

Moreover, the heights once taken, the flotilla would speedily be driven to the open water by the British guns. On the other hand it was of little advantage to deprive the American ships of the shelter of the batteries ashore, unless the British squadron were at hand to engage them. However, Sir George waited until the morning of the 7th, when perceiving that the American ships had taken up a new anchorage at a greater distance from the shore—beyond cannon-shot as he estimated—he summoned Downie to join him at once, if his squadron were fit for action, and set his men to erect batteries and siege-guns. Prevost's point—and his reasoning was perfectly sound— was that the American fleet and army were not within supporting distance of each other, and might be destroyed in detail.

Downie, who had already brought his ships to Lacolle, twenty-five miles north of Cumberland Bay, against wind and current, answered that it would be a day or two before the *Confiance* would be fit for action, but that no time would be lost, as he could employ the interval in working up to Chazy. On the 8th Prevost again wrote to Downie that he was only awaiting the arrival of the squadron to make his attack; and now Downie answered more curtly that the *Confiance* was still unready, and would remain at Chazy until his guns were mounted.

Meanwhile American militia streamed daily into Macomb's camp, augmenting his force and enabling him to strengthen his defences; and on the 9th Prevost sent a third nagging letter, acquitting Downie of all intentional delay but plainly revealing his own impatience, and stating that according to the reports of deserters the American fleet was inefficiently manned. Downie replied briefly that he should weigh at midnight, and expected to round into Cumberland Bay at dawn of the 10th, he added:

> In manning the flotilla and ships we are many short, I have made application to the officer commanding at Chazy for a company of the Thirty-Ninth to make up.

strongest of the American ships, and would, it was hoped, be ready for service in three weeks.

On the 30th Prevost inspected his first brigade at Chambly, and, proceeding on the 31st to Odell's Town, within a mile of the American frontier, heard there of Izard's march to Sackett's with four thousand men. This unlooked-for piece of intelligence decided him to advance at once without waiting for the co-operation of the fleet, in the hope of forcing Izard to return and of thus making a diversion in Drummond's favour.

Accordingly crossing the frontier he, on the 3rd of September, occupied an entrenched camp at Champlain on the Great Chazy, which was abandoned by the enemy at his approach, and on the 4th moved on to the Little Chazy, where his supplies were to be landed. Here he saw the naval commander, Captain Downie, who assured him that the flotilla would be ready to co-operate with the army within forty-eight hours, and that, from all that he could ascertain concerning the American squadron, there need be little misgiving as to the issue of a naval action.

On the 6th, therefore, Prevost advanced in two columns to Plattsburg, a march of twelve miles only, but rendered laborious by the obstruction of felled trees and ruined bridges, with which the American commander sought to impede his progress. Some attempt was made to induce the American militia to offer resistance, but in vain, the British columns brushing them contemptuously aside without even condescending to deploy. By the afternoon the entire force of the enemy had retreated to a strongly fortified position on the south side of the River Saranac.

It is said that Prevost proposed to attack the works immediately, but desisted upon the representation that one of his brigades was too much fatigued by a rapid march from Chazy to be fit for immediate action, (*Life of Sir George Prevost*). If so, it was a pity that he did not act upon his opinion at all risks. The departure of Izard had left his successor, General Macomb, with only fifteen hundred effective regular troops and about the same number of recruits and convalescents; and to this scanty force only seven hundred dispirited militia had as yet been added. (Izard said that he had left 3000 regular troops at Plattsburg).

Prevost himself had some eleven thousand men, most of them of the finest quality; and one half of them should certainly have sufficed to sweep the enemy away. The Saranac itself was fordable; and

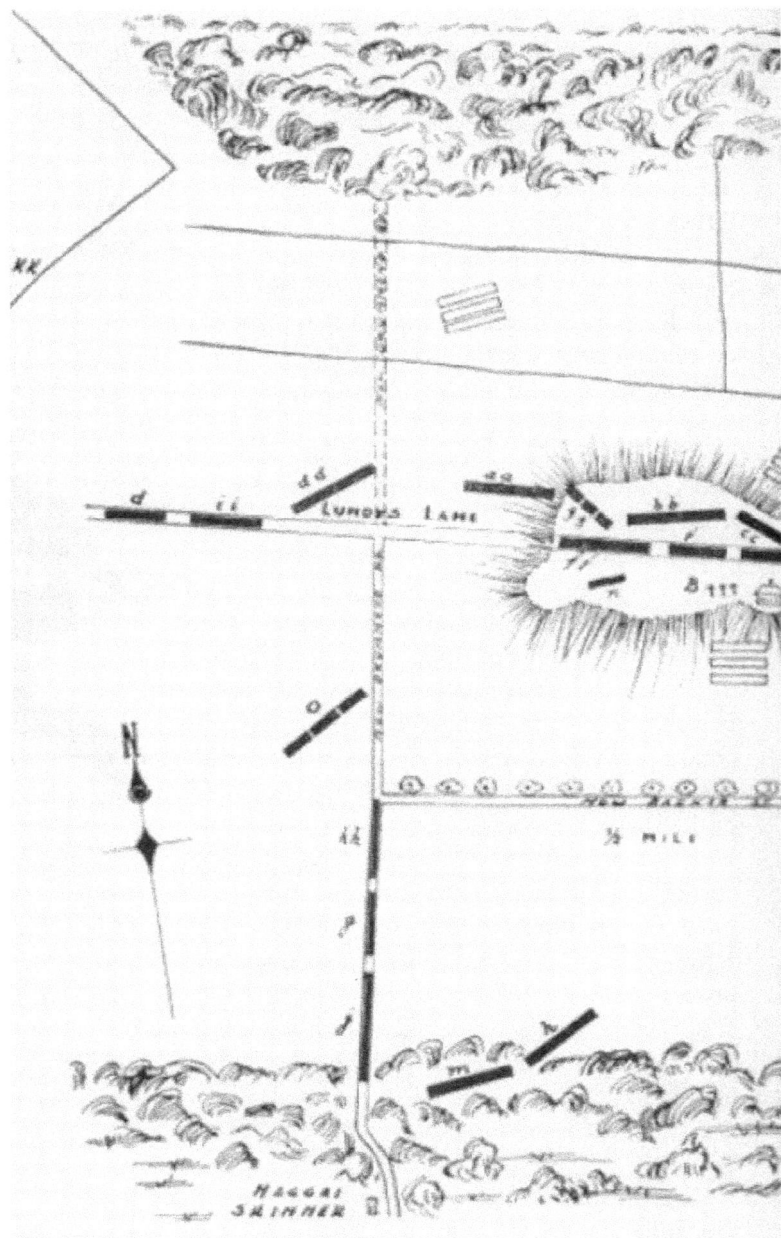

KK

LUNDYS LANE

d   ii   dd

aa
bb
cc
ff
n   B

o

N

kk

g

j

l

m

½ MILE

HAGGAI
SKINNER

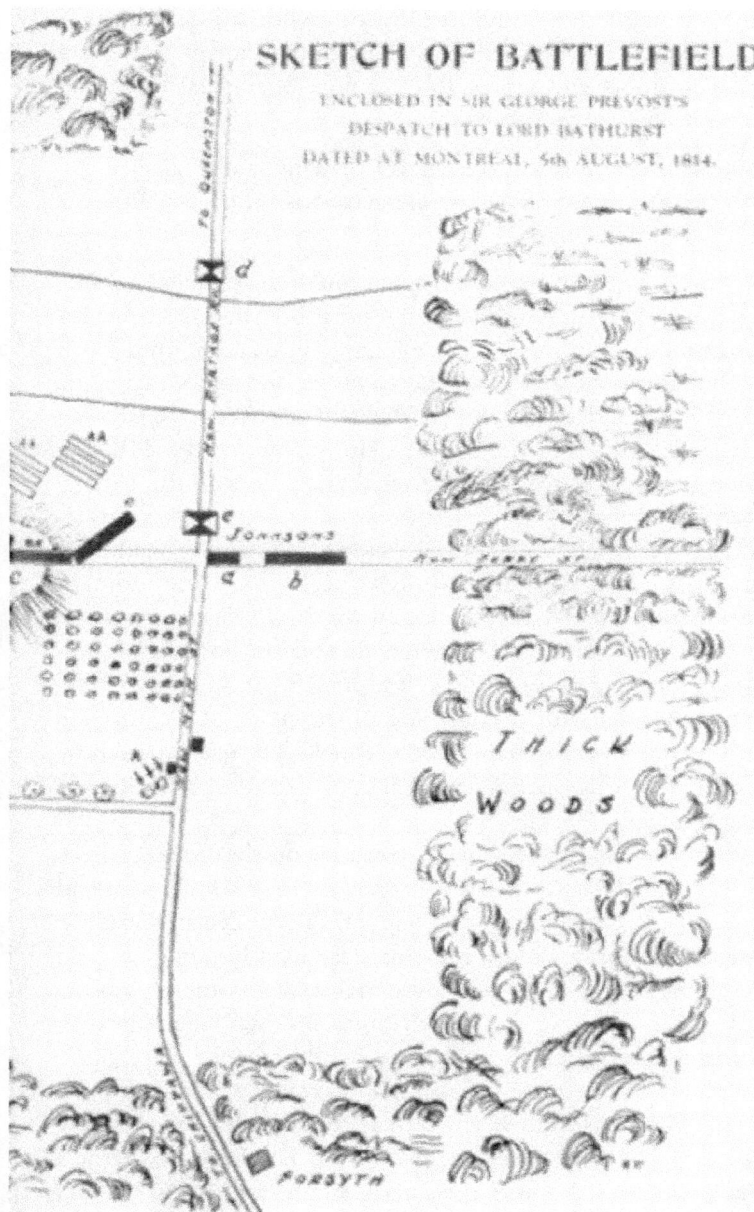

SKETCH OF BATTLEFIELD

ENCLOSED IN SIR GEORGE PREVOST'S
DESPATCH TO LORD BATHURST
DATED AT MONTREAL, 5th AUGUST, 1814.

The company was supplied, strange to its work, strange to the officers, strange to everything; but a strong head wind prevented the squadron from making any way; and Prevost, who had held his columns in readiness to storm since six o'clock in the morning, was fain to withdraw his troops and address to Downie a fourth irritating letter expressive of his disappointment:

> I ascribe it to the unfortunate change of wind, and I shall rejoice to learn from you that my expectations have been frustrated by no other cause.

Greatly hurt by this undeserved imputation of dilatoriness, Downie answered verbally to Prevost's messenger that he was responsible for the squadron and did not mean it to be hurried into action until it was fit to fight; but, speaking later in the day to his second in command, he declared that he intended to convince the general that the naval force would not be backward in the attack. Before dawn of the 11th the squadron weighed anchor with a fair wind and stood up the narrow channel towards the lake.

In his last letter to Downie, Prevost stated that his troops had been held ready to storm the enemy's works at nearly the same moment as the naval action should commence in the bay. "Nearly the same moment" is a vague phrase, but Downie after verbal communication with Prevost's messengers understood it to mean that the army would assault simultaneously with the opening of the naval attack, that the American squadron would thereby be compelled to quit its anchorage, and that in the consequent confusion the British ships would have a decided advantage.

Prevost had thrown up two heavy batteries on the shore to keep the American gun-boats at a distance in case they should stand in to annoy his flank; but if, as he maintained, the American squadron was out of range from his guns, it is not clear why his attack should cause the ships to move. If he should master Macomb's position, which was nearer to the hostile fleet than was his own, he might turn the American heavy ordnance, which he would capture there, upon them; though even then it is uncertain whether they would have been within range. Thus it is not clear whether Prevost intended the navy to help the army, or the army to help the navy. But beyond question he was working above all things for a naval victory; and, from the fact that Downie was instructed to announce his approach by a discharge of signal guns, it would be reasonable to conclude that the attack on land was to precede that on water.

At five o'clock in the morning Downie fired his signal guns, and, heaving to at 7.30 near the entrance to Cumberland Bay, went forward in a boat to reconnoitre the enemy's squadron. This was anchored in single line ahead north and south across the middle of the bay, with all the skill that was to be expected from its brave and capable commander, Commodore Macdonough. Downie then made his dispositions to engage the enemy, and, rounding Cumberland Head at about nine o'clock, stood into the bay.

Prevost, meanwhile, guessing that a fair wind would certainly bring the British squadron into action, visited his second in command at daybreak, and directed the troops to cook their breakfast and to be ready for the assault. Simultaneously with the opening of fire by Downie, Prevost's batteries engaged and silenced the only American battery that bore upon the water. Orders were sent to the brigades of Robinson and Power to move down under cover of the forest to a ford wide on the left of the American position, and to Brisbane's brigade to approach the bridge opposite to the enemy's centre.

Robinson and Power accordingly set their battalions in motion, but, being misled by their guide, were obliged to counter-march, and thus lost at least an hour in arriving at their point of action. They then forced the ford, and were in the act of advancing through the wood, when a message arrived from Prevost to break off the engagement and to retire.

The reason for this sudden order was cogent. The squadron under Downie's orders after two hours and a quarter of incessant fighting had been totally defeated. Downie himself had been killed in the first few minutes of the action; his second in command was a prisoner, and his flagship had hauled down her flag in a sinking condition. In the circumstances Prevost rightly judged it useless waste of life to persist in his attack, and decided to fall back at once. Without a fleet any military advantage would have been worthless, and every day's delay would have made his position more difficult. Desertion, always considerable in America owing to the temptation offered by American agents, was increasing. Provisions were scanty and, owing to the failure of water-transport, likely to become scantier.

The only roads lay through swamps, and, by reason of the weather and the obstructions made by the enemy, were almost impassable. Lastly, the American militia was gathering in masses all round the British. Prevost, therefore, with sound judgment retreated on the 12th, abandoning a certain quantity of stores which he had no means of removing. His casualties during the advance, the action and the subsequent retreat amounted to twenty officers and two hundred and twenty-three men killed, wounded and missing.

The navy was furious at this mishap, and raised such an outcry against Prevost that he was recalled to be tried by court-martial. The gist of the charge against him was that he had hurried the fleet into battle before it was ready, in disadvantageous circumstances, and for no particular object; and that he had upset the whole of Downie's arrangements by failing to make his attack at the concerted time. It is certain that the *Confiance*, still uncompleted, and with an untrained crew that had not spent even a week together to enable them to know their officers and each other, was unready for action.

It is certain also that Downie, whether Prevost intended it or not, had interpreted the General's last letter as an insinuation of backwardness on the part of the navy. It is quite possible that Prevost designed this missive to be a spur only and not a taunt; nor is it surprising if he did think the naval service somewhat dilatory, for Yeo had lost the whole of the campaigning season on Lake Ontario by the delay in fitting out the *St. Lawrence*, and Downie seemed likely to lose it on Lake Champlain through his slowness in equipping the *Confiance*.

That the naval officers can be held responsible for such delay is, however, in the highest degree doubtful; and so far Prevost may be blamed for putting undue pressure upon Downie. As a military officer the general was quite incompetent to pronounce whether a ship was or was not ready for immediate service, and upon such a point he should certainly have deferred to the representations of the naval commander. It must be admitted also that Downie's squadron, though superior to Macdonough's in the open, was inferior when attacking the Americans in a carefully selected defensive position. But that Downie's defeat was due to Prevost's failure to attack the American entrenchments ashore seems to me a proposition that cannot be maintained.

The whole issue turns upon the question whether Macdonough could be compelled by any of the batteries, American or British, upon the shore to weigh anchor and shift position, or, in other words, whether his squadron was or was not anchored within cannon-shot of the land. Careful enquiry was made of the American commanders, with a view to Prevost's trial, and Macomb answered unequivocally in the negative. Macdonough stated that his squadron lay a mile and a half from the batteries; and, as he moved out from a station closer inshore on the night of the 6th, it is a reasonable inference that he considered a mile and a half to be a safe distance.

Whatever may be said to the contrary, it is inconceivable that a prudent and capable commander, such as Macdonough was, should deliberately have taken up an anchorage from which he might be driven, to all intent at his enemy's own good time, into the jaws of a superior fleet. (I am aware that in holding this opinion I differ from so great an authority as the late Admiral Mahan; but his reasoning does not convince me).

This being so, it is evident that, whether misled by Prevost's staff-officers or not, Downie completely misconceived the situation. The whole affair seems to have been the outcome of a most unfortunate misunderstanding, due principally to the inability of the naval and military commanders to grasp each the limits of the other's capabilities.

There was, however, another reason for the indignation of the naval service against Prevost. In the rival squadrons the forces were about equal. In each there was a flagship of superior size, the British *Confiance* and the American *Saratoga*, three smaller vessels and eleven gunboats. Downie's dispositions appear to have been able enough, but at the critical moment of entering into action the wind failed, with consequences which were disastrous. The *Confiance* was compelled to anchor before she had reached her appointed station; the American galleys, being propelled by oars, were enabled to concentrate their fire upon her; and the *Finch*, one of the smaller British vessels, was unable to reach her place in the line and drifted ashore upon Crab Island, a mile to southward.

All this was sheer bad luck, the fortune of war. But the *Chub*, another small British vessel, on receiving some damage to her spars, was allowed by her commander to drift helplessly through the American line, where she hauled down her colours; and seven if not eight out of the eleven British gunboats, following the example of the officer in charge of them, turned tail directly the firing began. Thus the *Confiance* and the *Linnet* were left to carry on the fight practically alone, which they did with signal gallantry until overpowered.

Macdonough said to Lieutenant Robertson, Downie's successor, when the British officer surrendered his sword:

You owe it, sir, to the shameful conduct of your gun-boats and cutters that you are performing this office to me, for had they done their duty, you must have perceived from the situation of the *Saratoga* that I could hold out no longer.

The commander of the *Chub* was severely reprimanded by the court-martial which tried the officers and crews of the squadron in England, and the commander of the gun-boats absconded rather than face the consequences of his misconduct.

It is difficult to know whether to urge these circumstances in accusation or in defence of Prevost. On the one hand, it seems certain that the British squadron, properly manned and directed, could and would have beaten Macdonough's, and that it failed very much owing to the misconduct of both men and officers. On the other, it is impossible to believe that the gunboats would have behaved so ill as they did, had not their crews consisted principally of Canadian militia, imperfectly disciplined for any purpose, and little stiffened by a small leaven of soldiers and marines. Downie made no complaint of them that I can discover; but an officer of any spirit will never raise difficulties, and he may well have trusted to the general superiority of the *Confiance* to make good all defects.

Prevost died before he could stand his trial and, in default of his appearance, judgment has been given against him. This is very unfair. The whole weight of civil as well as of military direction lay upon him, and throughout the three wearing years of his command he was called upon to make bricks without straw. At the outset he was bidden to do his best without hope of troops or of money; and, though he received more of both than could have been expected, he never received them at the appointed time, and thus was unable to lay his plans with any certainty of being able to execute them.

Above all, he had no naval force, for but few officers and men could be spared from England; and yet this war was to all intent a naval war inland. Hence his instinct was to husband his resources, to stand constantly on the defensive, and to welcome every chance of an accommodation; and it cannot be said that such policy was altogether incorrect. It was unwise, indeed, to trust to any negotiation or agreement with the Americans, for, whatever the good faith of the individual officer who might treat with him, no confidence could be reposed in that of the President or of Congress. But the defensive attitude was the right one in principle, and was repeatedly approved by Wellington when his advice was sought.

It is easy to blame Prevost, and indeed Wellington also, for not taking advantage of offensive successes; but it must be remembered that Sir George had only imperfect and irregular information of events in Europe, and that he had to treat his force as the only army that existed for the defence of Canada. On the whole it must be said, taking his civil and military administration together, that he fulfilled an extremely difficult duty with no small measure of success, amid endless worry and anxiety, and latterly, as it should seem, though he was not yet fifty years of age, under the burden of failing health. When all is said, the criticism levelled at Prevost rarely rises above the natural but superficial cavilling of local and personal prejudice, and never regards the situation in its entirety. Yet his is, above all, a case in which it must be remembered that, though subordinates may reap the credit for any local success, the responsibility for every failure everywhere recoils upon the commander-in-chief.

The ablest and soberest of the American historians has written that the Battle of Lake Champlain, more than any other incident of the American War, deserves the epithet decisive. In a sense this is true, so far as concerns any efforts of the British Government to attempt an offensive movement on the Canadian frontier. In the first alarm after the defeat at Plattsburg, Liverpool offered the command in Canada to Wellington, in the hope that he might obtain peace upon honourable terms. Wellington put forward no objection, but said bluntly that he could promise himself little success, he wrote:

That which appears to me to be wanting, is not a general or general officers or troops, but a naval superiority on the lakes... This question is whether we shall acquire this naval superiority. If we can't, I shall do you but little good in America, and I shall go there only to prove the truth of Prevost's defence.

He added a few days later:

Does it not occur to you, that by appointing me to go to America at this moment, you give ground for belief all over Europe that your affairs there are in a much worse situation than they really are?—*Supp. Desp.* vol. ix. Wellington to Liverpool, 9th–18th Nov. 1814.

Here the great duke's strong common sense gave him insight into the heart of the matter. No object was to be gained by continuance of the war; and, in a contest of shipbuilding on the lakes, the natural advantages enjoyed by the Americans were so great that British superiority, though existent for the moment on Lake Ontario, was so precarious that its endurance could not be counted upon even from month to month. At best, therefore, England could obtain only a temporary and superficial success, which might or might not be useful for purposes of negotiation; whereas all essential profit had been gained already. Wellington wrote in one of the letters above quoted:

> Considering everything, it is my opinion that the war has been a successful one, and highly honourable to the British arms.

This was no exaggeration, but the strict and simple truth. The Americans had won two great naval victories on the lakes; but here was nothing very extraordinary, seeing that the naval resources of England were already taxed to the utmost by operations against France and the United States on the high seas; whereas America had at her command a large reserve of artificers and seamen from her maritime population. Even so, her chief naval commander, Chauncey, though by no means without talent and energy for organisation, had not shone in the field of active operations. Indeed it cost Perry and Macdonough, both excellent officers, no small effort to cope with the ill-manned and ill-equipped squadrons of Barclay and Downie.

On land also the Americans were not without their victories, most notably against the worst of the British commanders, Proctor; but, speaking broadly, the quality of their troops, the leadership of their generals, and the strategy of their government were one and all beneath contempt. After three campaigns they had indeed succeeded in mastering Detroit; but they failed to take the petty station of Mackinaw, they could establish no footing on the frontier of Niagara, and they were actually unable to expel the British from Fort Niagara on their own side of the boundary.

Considering the enormous resources of the United States and the powerlessness of England, locked as she was in a grapple with France for life or death, to send help to Canada, the war was, as said Wellington, successful and highly honourable to the British arms. The inevitable inference is that it was disgraceful to America; and so in fact it was; not because brave men were lacking in the United States—far from that—but because both government and people conceived of war not as the highest of human trials, to be encountered only after much searching of heart and prolonged training in discipline and endurance, but as an easy and triumphant progress, to be varied by the recreation of wanton mischief and plunder.

On the Canadian frontier the British could do little more than render nugatory the operations of the American forces; and this they successfully did, for it may truly be said that in that quarter the Americans in three campaigns accomplished absolutely nothing towards their avowed end, the conquest of Canada. It is now time to turn to the desultory operations in other districts, whereby the British sought to bring home to the Americans the fact that he who makes war must expect not only to give but to receive a buffet.

CHAPTER 4

Minor Operations in America

The first, though not the earliest in date, of the subsidiary offensive operations of the British was an expedition conducted by Sir John Sherbrooke, Lieutenant-Governor of Nova Scotia, with the view of occupying so much of the State of Maine as should ensure uninterrupted communication between Halifax and Quebec. Sherbrooke sailed from Halifax on the 22nd of August with ten transports containing nearly two thousand men, (Dets. of 29th, 7/60th, 62nd and 98th); and, escorted by a squadron under Admiral Griffith, made for the Penobscot River, which he entered on the 1st of September.

Having taken the fort of Castine after a trifling resistance, Sherbrooke on the 3rd sent a detachment farther up the stream. These drove away after a slight skirmish a force of militia, which was endeavouring to protect an American frigate, and, after forcing the enemy to abandon and burn the frigate, followed up the militia and compelled them to disperse. On the 9th the expedition dropped down the river again to Machias, when the fort was evacuated upon the approach of the British; and Sherbrooke, having annexed by proclamation all the country lying east of the Penobscot up to the boundary of New Brunswick, settled down to occupy it with the full consent of the inhabitants.

Upon Wellington's representations, however, England renounced all claim to keep this territory upon the negotiations for peace. Wellington contended, truly enough, that Sherbrooke's garrison was so small that it could not claim possession; but it was none the less a misfortune that the new boundary could not have been preserved, for it might have averted dangerous discontent and disputes in the future.

Far more effective in its results was the armament which descended in August upon the Chesapeake, the happy hunting-ground of the

British fleet during the year 1813. The only defensive force kept by the American Government in this quarter was a flotilla of thirteen galleys and gun-boats under Commodore Barney, which, owing to their lighter draught, were able to escape up the rivers if seriously threatened. Barney was a brave and skilful officer, but his operations were cramped by the fact that the British had established and fortified an advanced base at Tangier Island opposite the mouth of the Potomac, from which their ships effectually hindered the passage of the flotilla between the five great rivers—the Patuxent, Potomac, Rappahannock, York and James, that run into the southern portion of Chesapeake Bay.

At the confluence of the Potomac with its tributary, the Eastern Branch, stands the city of Washington, which, as the capital of the United States, the British Government had selected as the fittest recipient of a first salutary lesson. The Americans had wantonly wrecked and plundered York, the capital of Upper Canada; they were now to have an opportunity of defending their own chief city. On the 1st of June General Ross had sailed from Bordeaux with three battalions, (1/4th, 44th, 85th, the 44th sent home from Portugal early in 1813, had rejoined after the Battle of Toulouse), and one company of artillery from Wellington's army, and arrived at Bermuda on the 24th.

There he picked up the Twenty-First and a battalion of marines; and, proceeding on his voyage on the 3rd of August, entered the capes of the Chesapeake together with his convoy on the 15th. There were now assembled at the rendezvous four ships of the line, and several smaller vessels of war, from which the naval commander in chief, Sir Alexander Cochrane, furnished Ross with yet another battalion of seven hundred marines, raising his force to over four thousand men.

The first object of the expedition was the destruction of Barney's flotilla at the head of the Patuxent, from the banks of which river Washington also could be reached by a short march overland. The squadron of frigates was sent up the Potomac to keep the enemy in doubt as to the true route that would be taken by the army; and on the 18th the main body of the armament sailed up the windings of the Patuxent between banks covered with huge forest trees. On the 19th the troops were landed at Benedict, on the western margin of the river twenty-five miles from its mouth, and were organised by Ross into three brigades, one consisting of light troops under Colonel Thornton, the other two being under Colonels Brooke and Paterson. (See list following).

1st Brigade: Lt.-Col. Thornton (85th): 85th L.I., light cos. of 4th, 21st, and 44th; 1 co. marines; 1 co. negroes.

2nd Brigade: Lt.-Col. Brooke (4th): 4th, 44th.

3rd Brigade: Lt.-Col. Paterson (21st): 21st, 1 batt. marines. Artillery: 1 six-pounder, 2 light three-pounders.

The force then advanced northward, keeping in touch with the squadron on the river, to Upper Marlborough, three miles above Pit Point, where Barney's flotilla was lying. Perceiving escape to be impossible the American Commodore withdrew his crews on the 21st, leaving only a few men upon each boat to set fire to her; and on the 22nd, upon the approach of the British vessels, the entire flotilla was destroyed.

From Upper Marlborough two roads led to Washington, the one bearing nearly due west to a bridge which carried it over the Eastern Branch immediately into the city, the other trending north-west to the bridge of Bladensburg, which lay about five miles farther up the river. About midway in the former of these roads was a crossway at a place called Oldfields, where roads forked out north-westward to Bladensburg, and south-west upon Fort Washington, which was the principal defence of the capital on the Potomac. There was thus considerable embarrassment for the American commander who was charged with the duty of repelling the invaders, for he could not divine which would be the objective preferred by his enemy nor, except in the case of Fort Washington, by what road he would decide to approach it.

The unfortunate individual selected for this trying duty was General Winder; and the force at his disposal amounted to between five to six thousand men, all of whom, with the exception of Barney's four hundred sailors, were militia. Winder had received his appointment on the 2nd day of July as military chief of a large district, which should have furnished him, according to the returns on paper, with ninety-three thousand militia. Had a force of even one-fourth of his strength been obtainable, however raw, it could have given Ross infinite trouble and perhaps have turned him back altogether; for the ground over which he had advanced was covered with forest, offering endless opportunities for the admirable markmanship of the American riflemen, and presenting at every step strong positions for defence.

So rotten, however, was the administrative system, and so slow were the people to answer the call of patriotic duty, that, out of fifteen thousand men summoned by the government, not above three thousand had come forward by the 22nd of August. More were indeed on the way; but with such puny numbers Winder had no alternative but to fall back, finally taking up a position at Oldfields, as the point which he rightly judged to be most important. As he had expected, Ross advanced by the western road, and at nightfall of the 23rd the British encamped within three miles of Oldfields. Dreading the effect of a possible night attack, Winder retired in the darkness to Washington, burning the bridges over the Eastern Branch behind him; whereupon Ross on the 24th turned north-westwards, and at noon marched into Bladensburg.

Contrary to Winder's orders some militia stationed at this point had been withdrawn by their officers across the river, though without destruction of the bridge, and had been formed on some heights astride the road to Washington on the right bank, facing east. On the summit was posted a battery, which commanded the bridge, and on each flank of the guns was an array of infantry, with a second line in support. Since, however, the stream was fordable in many places above the bridge, this second line was weakened in order to extend the American left, which was further strengthened, when Winder came up, by the guns that he brought with him.

The dispositions had not long been complete when the British Light Brigade topped the rising ground on the opposite side of the bridge; and though the Second and Third Brigades were still far in rear, the men being in bad condition after a long voyage, Thornton prepared to attack immediately. Ross assented; and at about one o'clock in the afternoon Thornton launched the Light Brigade at the bridge, and carried the passage, in spite of some loss from the American artillery.

At this moment Barney came up with his seamen and guns, which were posted by Winder astride of the road to Washington and opposite the bridge. While the commodore was making his dispositions, a few rockets thrown by the British towards the American left sufficed to throw the American militia in that quarter into panic, and the greater part of both lines turned and ran. A few only stood firm for a time, but broke immediately when Winder attempted to draw them back a little; and thus the American left was routed almost before it was engaged.

Presently Thornton, having re-formed his brigade after passing the bridge, advanced up the road, apparently without throwing out a single skirmisher, and finding Barney's battery before him, halted for a few minutes. The commodore coolly reserved his fire until Thornton was within close range, and then swept the British off the road with grape. A second and a third frontal attack were in like manner repulsed, and a fourth directed against Barney's right was met by a withering fire from three field-guns and from the musketry of the American seamen and marines.

By this time Thornton himself, the two field-officers and nine other officers of the Eighty-Fifth had fallen; and the Light Brigade was ordered to hold its own until Brooke's brigade could come up. In about half an hour, as it seems, Brooke appeared, his men much exhausted by a rapid march under a hot sun after long confinement on board ship. He was directed to turn the American right, while Ross galloped off to take personal command of the Light Brigade. By this time nearly the whole of the American force had disappeared from the field, with the exception of Barney's detachment and a body of five or six hundred infantry, which was very strongly posted upon his right.

Brooke led the Forty-Fourth against Barney's exposed left flank, and directed the Fourth to turn the infantry on the American right. These last after a feeble volley or two turned and ran before a charge of half their number of British; and Barney was left alone with his naval detachment, himself and two of his officers badly wounded, and two more of them killed. His men stood until some of them were bayoneted at their guns, when, finding that his ammunition-drivers had fled and that the whole party was in danger of capture, the commodore ordered them to save themselves. Ten guns and a few prisoners fell into Ross's hands, among the latter being Barney himself, who was deservedly treated by his captors with all possible consideration and cordiality. He and his little band of disciplined seamen and marines had covered themselves with honour.

The action, trifling though it was, appears to have been ill-managed by Ross, who hurried his troops into action piece-meal, and thus ran great and unnecessary risk of seeing them defeated in detail. If it be urged that time was a great object, the obvious answer is that Ross was obliged, after all, to await the arrival of Brooke's brigade before he could drive the Americans from their position. Thornton also appears to have handled his brigade without skill or science, delivering his frontal attacks in the most primitive and bludgeon-like fashion, with the inevitable consequence of temporary failure and appreciable loss.

The casualties of the British numbered two hundred and forty-nine; and, strong though the Americans were in artillery, this was more than should have been needed to displace four hundred disciplined men encumbered by a rabble of five thousand. Harry Smith, who was present, did not hesitate to say that John Colborne would have accomplished as much as Ross at the sacrifice of no more than fifty men. However, the victory was complete, though the casualties of the vanquished hardly exceeded fifty; and Ross, after a short halt resuming his advance, entered Washington at eight o'clock on the same evening.

In the morning Secretary Armstrong had ridden out to the American position with his colleagues, and had assured President Madison that, in a fight between regulars and militia, the militia must be beaten. None the less the President had prepared a supper of forty covers for his victorious officers; and this repast, to Madison's infinite mortification, was consumed by Ross and his staff.

Then the work of punishment began, scrupulously judicial but severe. Private property was respected, and plunder was most strictly forbidden; but all public buildings, including the President's official residence and the Parliament House, as well as the navy-yard, store-houses, barracks and arsenal, were burned to the ground. Such destruction, even in the way of reprisal, is revolting to the civilised human mind, and though rigorously executed in obedience to orders from Downing Street, was by no means to the taste of many of Wellington's officers.

The Americans of course shrieked loudly about vandalism, barbarism and so forth, and their cries were echoed by the ignoble faction which from beginning to end of the Great War sought to hamper the British Government and their country in the House of Commons. Nevertheless the punishment was righteous, and the Americans had only themselves to thank for it. York, the humble capital, but still the capital, of Upper Canada, had been treated by them in like fashion with far greater parade of wantonness and insolence; and both at York and in sundry villages private property had been destroyed and pillaged with the brutality peculiar to levies, which go eagerly afield to oppress the helpless, but fly to their own homes when they meet armed men. The burning of the public buildings at Washington was a salutary lesson to a nation whose conception of war was the bullying of a weaker neighbour.

The panic caused by this raid of four thousand enemies was complete. Five small British men-of-war, which had ascended the Potomac under command of Captain Gordon, while the main armament went up the Patuxent, arrived after infinite difficulty and exertion, owing to shoal waters, on the 27th before Fort Washington. The fort itself, which mounted seventeen heavy guns besides smaller ordnance, was basely abandoned by its commander at the bursting of the first British shell. Thereupon the town of Alexandria, situated five miles below Washington, made overtures of capitulation; and Gordon, after holding the town for three days, retired, taking with him a number of trading vessels fully loaded with merchandise.

Meanwhile Ross withdrew his troops from Washington on the night of the 25th; and on the 29th returned safe and unmolested to Benedict. He owed the tranquillity of his retirement, it seems, to the report assiduously circulated by himself that he was going next to Baltimore and Annapolis, upon which the Americans shifted all their troops to that quarter.

The naval commanders, always eager for operations ashore and still untaught by the lessons of Curaçoa, Vera Cruz, Cadiz and Ferrol, now became urgent for an attack upon Baltimore, not without hope, as was natural in those days, of a great haul of shipping and merchandise and consequently of prize-money.

Lieutenant De Lacy Evans, of Ross's staff, who later rose to some degree of military fame, seconded Admirals Cochrane and Cockburn; and only Harry Smith (if his own story is to be believed) uttered a note of warning. He represented that half of the men were on the sick list, owing to fatiguing marches after long confinement on board ship, that the enemy had been induced by Ross's own stratagem to concentrate force at Baltimore, and that the passage up the river to the city had been obstructed by sunken ships. Ross, before sending Smith home with despatches, promised to have nothing to do with the adventure; and apparently he prevailed for a time with the admirals, for Cochrane wrote on the 30th that the next enterprise attempted would be the reduction of Rhode Island with a view to quartering the army upon the enemy until November; after which, if reinforced, it would proceed southward.

On the 2nd of September this same project was still in favour, and the more so since the Americans would judge Rhode Island to be the base for a grand attack upon New York. They were in fact already fortifying Brooklyn and Manhattan Island, according to Cochrane's information, and would thus be unable to spare reinforcements for the Canadian frontier—an erroneous calculation, for there was New York militia both with Brown in his sortie from Fort Erie on the 17th, and with Macomb at Plattsburg on the 11th of September. However, for some reason which does not appear, the project against Baltimore was revived, and Ross was induced to consent to it. (W.O. i. Ross to Sec. of State, 30th Aug., 2nd Sept. 1814).

The troops were accordingly re-embarked; and the squadron, sailing up Chesapeake Bay, anchored at the mouth of the Patapsco River, which is the water-way to Baltimore Harbour, while the lighter vessels stood up the stream to the northern shore a little above North Point. Here on the morning of the 12th the soldiers were landed on the peninsula formed by the Back River on the north and the Patapsco on the south, at a point some thirteen miles from Baltimore.

Advancing northward to turn the head of an inlet, they came upon the enemy completing his entrenchments across a neck of land less than half a mile broad from water to water. This position was abandoned instantly on the approach of the red-coated skirmishers; and the British moved on for another two miles, when, entering wooded country, they found themselves much harassed by concealed American riflemen.

Ross, who was riding in advance to reconnoitre, was mortally wounded by one of these marksmen; but Brooke, taking command, pressed on to within five miles of Baltimore, when he was again stopped by some five thousand Americans with six guns, who were drawn up in dense formation across a second narrow neck of land, here more than a thousand yards wide. Brooke promptly sent out the Light Brigade in skirmishing order, deployed his own brigade along the whole length of the line, and held his third brigade in columns on the road, with orders to deploy to the left and press the American right as soon as the ground should become sufficiently open to permit the movement.

The water on the American left was fordable, and for this reason General Stricker, who commanded their force, had placed one battalion *en potence* at the extremity of his line, so as to guard his left flank. All being ready, Brooke launched his troops to the attack; and the Fourth, which had worked its way unseen close to Stricker's left, suddenly revealed itself within twenty yards of the battalion mentioned above. The Americans fired one random volley and fled; the whole of the left wing fled likewise; and though the right wing stood for a little longer and seems to have offered some real resistance, all presently ran away in the haste and confusion of panic, leaving two guns behind them.

The day being far spent, and the troops much fatigued by such exertions on their first day ashore, Brooke halted for the night where he stood, and on the following morning advanced to within a mile and a half of Baltimore. He found the ring of hills, which surrounded the city, strengthened by a chain of palisaded redoubts, which were connected by a small breastwork. These lines were defended, according to the information furnished to him, by some fifteen thousand militia with a considerable number of guns; wherefore, to neutralise the superiority of the enemy's artillery as far as possible, he resolved to delay his attack until the night. In the evening, however, he heard from Cochrane that the entrance to the harbour had been blocked by sunken ships, and that the navy was consequently unable to co-operate in any further movement.

This fact, as has been told, was known to the British commanders before they started on the expedition, but the admirals had made light of it, averring that they would remove all obstacles without difficulty. Brooke, therefore, retired slowly on the 14th, and, finding himself unpursued, re-embarked his soldiers at North Point. The operations had cost the British two hundred and ninety killed and wounded, of which ninety-two belonged to the Twenty-First, and ninety-nine to the Forty-Fourth—a useless and almost a wicked sacrifice of life, for no object except, it is to be feared, to bring prize-money to the navy. Unfortunately this was not the first nor the last disaster attributable to the same cause.

With a force now reduced to little more than thirty-five hundred men, Brooke, in company with Admiral Malcolm, made a petty raid on the Virginian side of the Potomac on the 5th and 6th of October; and then sailed for Jamaica, where he arrived on the 1st of November. There he was joined on the 21st by five companies of the Rifle Brigade, (3rd Batt., arrived at Plymouth from the Peninsula 18th of July), and by the Ninety-Third Highlanders, which had recently returned, the one from France and the other from the Cape of Good Hope.

Cochrane with his fleet having already arrived on the 19th, the armament was completed by the coming of two West India regiments, and presently sailed for the mouth of the Mississippi. Its destination, as was too often the case throughout this war, had already been proclaimed in the West Indian newspapers, and possibly was no secret in any quarter by the autumn of 1814. In May, very soon after taking over the command of the North American and West Indian stations,

Admiral Cochrane had despatched to the mouth of the Apalachicola River a frigate, whose captain, Pigot by name, after negotiation with the Creek and Choctaw Indians, had reported that, with the aid of a few British officers and sergeants, these savages could gain possession of Baton Rouge, from which base the conquest of New Orleans and the Lower Mississippi would be a simple matter.

Accordingly Cochrane in August had sent an officer and a few non-commissioned officers, together with arms and ammunition, to the Indians, and seconded Pigot's recommendation to the government in Downing Street. His views found all too ready acceptance with Ministers, who had already resolved to despatch a formidable force to New Orleans under Sir Rowland Hill.

✶✶✶✶✶✶

Sir John Hope had been selected first to command this expedition; and Hill was substituted in consequence of Sir John's capture before Bayonne. Wellington, *Supp. Desp.* ix. Sir G. Murray declined the offer of a divisional command in this force, *ibid.*

✶✶✶✶✶✶

As it happened, the political situation was not such as to permit the intended number of troops to be spared from Europe; and the expedition was therefore limited to six thousand men, of which one brigade, under Major-General Lambert, was to join the main body in the Mississippi itself. After the death of Ross, moreover, Sir Edward Pakenham, Wellington's brother-in-law, and lately his Adjutant -general, was appointed to the supreme command.

It is easy to see that the choice of New Orleans as an objective was due to naval advice, and that this advice was due chiefly to the desire for prize-money. The city was the great depot for the exportation of cotton and sugar; and it was estimated that the crops of these two commodities alone, stored up within it, were worth in England some three-and-a-half millions sterling, which tobacco, hemp, lead and shipping would increase to fully four millions.

The seizure of so rich a hoard, if it could be easily and cheaply effected, might conceivably be the most telling blow that England could strike at the United States, a country upon which it is notoriously difficult to inflict vital injury. But this was not the reason why the naval officers recommended it. Prize-money had for nearly two centuries been the motive for all amphibious operations recommended by the Navy; and this of New Orleans was no exception.

If any naval officers had shown stronger lust of prize than others, they were the Scots; and all three of the admirals engaged in this expedition—excellent men in their own profession—were by a singular coincidence Scotsmen, Cochrane, Cockburn and Malcolm. Cochrane at the outset estimated that three thousand British soldiers would suffice to drive the Americans entirely out of Louisiana, as they would be joined by all the Indians, disaffected French and Spaniards; a piece of folly so childish that it ought to have warned the British Ministers against listening to any of his projects. Listen they did, however, though in their instructions to the commanders they stated the objects of the expedition to be, first, the seizure of the mouth of the Mississippi, so as to deprive the American back-settlements of communication with the sea, and, next, the occupation of some valuable possessions which would be useful to hold in pledge against the negotiations for peace.

The general was also authorised to encourage any movement in favour of setting up an independent government in Louisiana and of restoring it to Spain; but at the same time to make it clearly understood that the British Government could not make such independence or transfer of allegiance an essential condition in the negotiations for peace. This policy was dangerously near akin to that which had made shipwreck of the British cause in South America.

On the 2nd of December General Jackson, who had lately commanded American troops in operations against the Creek Indians, arrived at New Orleans, where the militia of Kentucky and Tennessee had already received orders to join him by way of the river. He was a man who had gained some military experience in fighting against savages, a rancorous hater of the British, with whom he had combated as a boy in the war of the American Revolution, brave, shrewd, energetic and resolute. His determination, openly expressed from the beginning, to harass, torment and annoy the British invaders until they were expelled, shows that he rightly appreciated the problem set to him, and had thought out the best means for its solution.

On the 8th Cochrane anchored off Ship Island in Mississippi Sound, and began without delay to make his preparations. It was hopeless to think of sailing past the forts on the Lower Mississippi, and he therefore decided to turn those works by approaching the river through one or other of the creeks that traverse the huge swampy delta to east of it. From Ship Island the direct way was across the shallow lagoon called Lake Borgne, at the head of which a creek, known as the Bayou Bienvenu, furnished a landing-place within five miles of the Mississippi.

Five American gun-boats and a few smaller craft defended this lagoon; and, having no vessels of sufficiently light draught to navigate its waters, Cochrane was obliged to attack them with forty-five rowing boats of his fleet. This he did successfully on the 14th of December, capturing after a very sharp fight every one of the American vessels. The way being thus laid open, the advanced guard, (Cavalry. 14th L.D., dismounted; Advance. 4th, 85th, 95th; 1st Brigade. 21st, 44th, 5th W.I.R.; 2nd Brigade. 93rd, 7th W.I.R), was put into the ships' boats and rowed to Isle aux Poix, a wretched swampy islet at the mouth of the Pearl river, some twenty miles east of the intended place of ultimate debarkation.

Officers were sent forward to reconnoitre the Bayou Bienvenu, who found no sign of opposition to an advance by that line; and by the 21st the whole of the land forces were assembled at Isle aux Poix. On the morning of the 22nd General Keane and Admiral Malcolm embarked with twenty-four hundred men on gun-vessels and boats, and set sail for the mouth of the Bayou Bienvenu. Within three miles the largest vessels ran aground, and, as the voyage proceeded, the lagoon became dotted at intervals with craft which were hard and fast on the bottom; but none the less Keane and Malcolm pressed on, and after dark reached their appointed destination.

A company of the Rifles, seeing a light not far ahead upon the north bank, landed, and, advancing stealthily, surprised and captured an American picquet without the firing of a shot. They then occupied the captured post—a small artificial mound enclosed within a screen of reeds ten to twelve feet high, all springing out of a vast swamp. The leading boats rowed up the creek, always through a forest of reeds, and the soldiers disembarking on the south bank found themselves within seven miles of New Orleans. One by one the rest of the flotilla came up; and early on the 23rd sixteen hundred men were ashore, and marching for the river. At the head of the creek the ground was firmer; the reeds disappeared; forests of cypress took their place, then sugar-canes, orange groves, cultivation and houses.

After some trouble the situation of New Orleans was discovered, and the road to it; but the little party groped its way silently southward, hugging the banks of the creeks, which furnished the only stable ground for their feet, and so penetrating at about eleven o'clock to the house of a Mr. Villeré. Here a second picquet was surprised and captured, with however the unfortunate exception of an officer, who contrived to escape and give the alarm at New Orleans.

Thus far all had gone well; and the surprise of two picquets immediately after the destruction of the American flotilla did no great credit to Jackson's vigilance. But the strain upon the men of both services had been very heavy. The unfortunate bluejackets had been in the boats for eight unbroken days and nights, tugging almost continuously at the oar; and some of the soldiers had been cooped up likewise for six days and nights.

Furthermore, shortly after the flotilla left Isle aux Poix, the rain fell in torrents, and ceased only to give way to a cutting north wind, sleet and ice. The boats were so much crowded that the soldiers had no room to move, but were compelled to sit still, cramped and half-frozen, for twelve, eighteen and almost twenty-four hours together. Yet not a word of complaint was heard either from the overwrought sailors nor from their comrades of the army; though it must have occurred at any rate to the blue-jackets that an expedition of such a nature could not be of long continuance.

The exertions and hardships of the previous thirty-six hours had served to bring up but one-third of the army. The boats had already returned to convey the two remaining brigades; but even then all supplies and stores would require to be transported in the same way—that is to say in row-boats—over a distance of seventy or eighty miles from Ship Island to the landing-place in the Bayou Bienvenu. Moreover, in case of defeat not only would re-embarkation of any kind be most difficult and hazardous, but it would be impossible to find sufficient small craft to carry the whole of the military force at once. There are times and circumstances in which such risks must and should be taken by commanders; but to put the country to the expense of sending six thousand men across the Atlantic for so mad a venture was little short of criminal.

The Spanish fishermen, who had guided Keane and Malcolm on their way, pressed them to advance at once. They urged with some measure of truth that Jackson's peremptory measures had made him unpopular in New Orleans, that the defences which he had raised so far were trifling, that he had no troops worth speaking of to hold them, and that the bulk of the population of the city would side with the invaders. Moreover it was not much past noon, and five hours of daylight would suffice for the work in hand. Had Keane realised, as he ought, that he was engaged not upon a military operation but upon a mere buccaneering adventure, he would have acted upon this advice.

The troops, set down as they were in the midst of chilly, unhealthy swamps after their long and miserable exposure in the boats, were sure to become sickly; and delay would permit his enemies to improve their earthworks and to collect fresh levies. At best he might achieve a daring and striking success; at worst he would sacrifice no more than a small detachment, whose defeat would indeed mean the ruin of the expedition—in itself no misfortune—but could hardly be reckoned a great disgrace. However, treating affairs seriously as he did, he pointed to his men still out of condition after a long voyage, to his supports, supplies, and means of retreat, all of them eighty miles away, and declined, in spite of the remonstrances of Admiral Cochrane and Colonel Thornton, to take the risk. Had he advanced at once, he would probably have surprised Jackson before the American concentration had been accomplished.

Jackson had been apprised on the morning of the 23rd of the arrival of a hostile flotilla at the head of Lake Borgne; but it was not until two in the afternoon that he learned of the disembarkation of the British and fired the alarm-gun. The only field-works so far constructed appear to have been an unfinished battery for two guns thrown up on the road, along the left bank of the Mississippi, that led to New Orleans, and its function was to flank one of the many broad ditches that traversed the narrow isthmus, which, pent in between cypress-swamps on the north and the great river on the south, gave access to the city from the east.

This line was held by three hundred and fifty militia, who, upon the news of the British landing, had demanded to be led against the enemy, but had wisely been restrained by their commander, who was probably shrewd enough to know that raw levies, who clamour for action, invariably run away under fire and generally shoot their leaders. The numbers of the Americans were too small to guard effectually a front of a thousand yards; and the ditch itself, though broad, could either have been crossed upon planks, of which there were plenty at hand, or could even in places have been forded.

The obstacle therefore might have been carried with little difficulty; and, if this had been done by one o'clock, New Orleans could have been reached by three or a little later. At that hour there were under Jackson's hand some nine hundred regular infantry, marines and artillery, with two guns, and perhaps three hundred volunteers. Seven to eight hundred more volunteers and militia were within call, but could not have arrived before four o'clock at the very earliest, probably not until half an hour later. There were a couple of small ships of war, the

Louisiana and the *Carolina*, at anchor within sight of the British, but their commanders and men were engaged in throwing up batteries to the north of the city to fend off an attack from Lake Pontchartrain; and it is doubtful whether they could have been in position to rake the flank of the British advance until too late.

Thus, if Keane had moved forward promptly, he would have found no regular scheme of resistance organised to meet him; and, though he must have approached the city through a long straggling suburb, where riflemen might have wrought great havoc among his troops, he should with ordinary good fortune have succeeded in overcoming all opposition. Jackson, however, was a man who would have fought to the last, and was quite prepared to set fire to New Orleans if he could not hold it.

Having resolved to halt, Keane allowed his weary soldiers to lounge about at their ease. The weather had become soft and mild, and men and officers wandered away to the neighbouring houses in search of food and wine, wherewith they comforted themselves, though to no excess, after a long fast and the hardships of the previous forty-eight hours. In the presence of so cunning an enemy, renowned for marksmanship and for skill in all the minor tricks of war, this seems imprudent; but, except for the advance of a few mounted riflemen, who were at once driven back by the foremost picquets, the Americans made no attempt to molest the British.

Such was Keane's confidence that, though aware of the presence of the two men-of-war in the river, he raised no shelter to shield his bivouac from a cannonade from the river, nor did he attempt to fortify his position against any attack either from the water or from the land. Night fell; the bivouac was ablaze with fires; and the men were asleep or cooking. Then suddenly round-shot came pouring among them from the side of the river, and a continuous roar, with the sight of distant flashes, proclaimed that one of the American ships had dropped down the river to a point over against Keane's headquarters, and was pouring in her broadsides as fast as they could be fired.

The panic and confusion became indescribable. The ground most heavily scored by the American shot was the alarm post around Keane's quarters, and thus the centre of command and the appointed rallying-place became the place of greatest danger. The foremost picquet of riflemen on the New Orleans road, under Captain Hallen, stuck to their post totally unmoved by the firing; the second picquet of the Eighty-Fifth, which was ensconced in a house and a garden somewhat to Hallen's right rear, succumbed to the panic and ran back to the bivouac. After vainly trying to array themselves in some kind of formation, officers and men finally took refuge under shelter of the raised bank of the river, or of any other cover that they could find, and there sorted themselves into a semblance of order.

The confusion was at its height when a dropping fire of musketry began opposite to Hallen's picquet. Jackson by five o'clock in the evening had collected some two thousand men, of which he had directed about fifteen hundred—including the whole of his regular troops—with two guns to assail the British front near the river, under his personal command; while five to six hundred more under General Coffee should fetch a compass, following the border of the cypress swamp, and fall upon Keane's right flank. The fire of the *Carolina's* guns was to be the signal for the attack, and, so far as Jackson's own force was concerned, the sloop opened at the right moment; but Coffee's column was still far from its appointed station when the American advanced guard first exchanged shots with Hallen's eighty riflemen.

Few though they were and unsupported, this little band of green-jackets held their post with desperate tenacity and would not give way. Strive as they might, the Americans could not force their way past them by the main road, for which reason, swerving to their left, they made their way across country athwart the British right, and occupied the house that had been evacuated by the picquet of the Eighty-Fifth. Thence penetrating eastward they came upon more companies of the Rifles and of the Eighty-Fifth, and engaged with these in a blind and confused struggle.

As both sides spoke the same language, not even voices could distinguish friends from foes in the darkness. British fired on British, and Americans upon Americans. Both sides made prisoners of their own men, discovered their mistake, and turned to seek their real foes. Where they met there were savage encounters with the bayonet and the butt, without order, without method, and with no clear object. Once the Americans obtained for a, moment possession of the road in rear of Hallen, and captured a reinforcement of thirty men who were on their way to him, but even so they could not drive him from his post. Gradually, as Coffee's column came into action, the enemy spread down the whole length of the British right flank, and the British position was enclosed in a triangle of fire, Hallen marking the apex, the *Carolina* the riverward side, and a stream of musketry the landward side.

In one spot the riflemen of the two nations stood almost muzzle to muzzle on each side of a light paling; in another the two light three-pounders, which were Keane's only artillery, stood silent, the officer in charge of them not daring to fire and hardly knowing which was his front and which his rear; in a third the British were pressing hard upon the two American cannon, and only with difficulty were driven back.

Gradually superior discipline and experience told. Some companies of the Twenty-First and Ninety-Third, which had first landed, stayed the progress of the enemy round the British right flank, and the Americans began to give way. The Eighty-Fifth recovered the house and garden abandoned by their picquet; and the Americans, losing heart as they lost ground, appear finally to have streamed back to New Orleans as a disorderly rabble. The fight had lasted for the best part of three hours; and at midnight all firing ceased.

The British loss in this affair amounted to two hundred and thirteen killed and wounded, and sixty-four prisoners. The brunt of the work had fallen upon the Eighty-Fifth and Ninety-Fifth, each of which counted over eighty officers and men slain or hurt, their joint casualties amounting to two hundred and twenty-eight killed, wounded and missing. The Americans lost two hundred and thirteen of all ranks, of whom seventy-four were prisoners. Upon striking the balance of advantage from these figures, therefore, the Americans may be said to have come off the better; and Jackson certainly deserved success from the promptness and vigour of his attack.

It is perhaps hardly too much to say that, if he had not encountered Hallen's handful of veterans from the Light Division upon the main road, he would have gone near to destroy one half, if not the whole, of Keane's detachment. Too much credit cannot be given to this little party of the Ninety-Fifth; and it is distressing to hear that Hallen, who was severely wounded on this occasion, was still a captain in 1824, when he retired from the army. By his good service principally the impetus of Jackson's onslaught was broken; and, in spite of that General's utmost personal exertions, the American troops were so much shaken by their repulse that, if the narratives of British officers are to be trusted, they could have offered little resistance to an immediate advance.

According to American accounts Jackson intended in concert with Coffee to renew the attack at one o'clock in the morning of the 24th, having been reinforced by a party of militia, but countermanded his

BATTLE OF NEW ORLEANS

orders upon learning that part of Brooke's brigade had arrived, and that the rest of it was following. Be that as it may—and Jackson's character was not such as to belie the story—the American general at four o'clock ordered a general retreat, and withdrew to the line of the canal, which was flanked by the two-gun battery already mentioned, three miles from the British bivouac and four miles below New Orleans.

Keane for his part remained supine. Whether or not a bold advance would have carried him straight into the city, it is difficult to say, but certain it is that he made no such attempt. At dawn of the 24th the *Carolina* was still firing upon the British lines, and she continued to do so at intervals for the rest of the day. Had Keane moved up to his right to outflank the American works, so as at least to secure the two-gun battery, which was open in rear, and to force Jackson to take up a position closer to the city, he might at any rate have withdrawn his troops during daylight beyond range of the *Carolina's* guns, and possibly have turned the captured American pieces upon her. But whether he was unnerved, or dared not take the responsibility upon himself when his commander-in-chief was hourly expected, he sat perfectly still.

On the 25th Jackson began to fortify his position in earnest, prolonging the broad ditch which already traversed the plain across the road to the Mississippi, a little in rear of the battery, and erecting a barricade of sugar-casks behind the ditch itself from the river to the cypress-swamp, to serve for a breastwork. The guns in the battery were also augmented to four heavy pieces which, raking the ditch from end to end, greatly increased its efficacy as an obstacle. Keane, no more than a mile and a half away, allowed the Americans to pursue this work without the slightest molestation, although by this time the whole strength of the force, excepting Lambert's brigade, had disembarked. Sir Edward Pakenham likewise arrived, full of apprehensions, for he distrusted Cochrane and had been most anxious to take up his command before operations should have been begun.

When he realised the situation into which the admiral had decoyed the army, he was with good reason furious. To all intent his force was cooped up on an isthmus three-quarters of a mile broad between the Mississippi and the swamp. In front was Jackson's fortified position; on the river were the enemy's armed vessels, flanking the only possible line of advance; and in rear were the lake and the sea. The only base of supply was some eighty miles distant, and accessible only in open boats; and the last four miles of this water-way were so narrow that

BATTLE OF NEW ORLEANS

it would hardly admit two boats abreast. When water-carriage ceased, the track from the landing-place to the camp—a distance of about four miles—was so bad after rains or high tides that provisions and stores could only be brought forward upon men's backs.

Moreover, victuals, with the exception of a few cattle, were unobtainable upon the spot, and the total quantity of supplies in the fleet did not exceed one month's store, which, taking the return voyage into account, was none too great. Again the line of communication was insecure; for five miles north of New Orleans was Lake Pontchartrain, from which there was an outlet into Lake Borgne. The squadron could not provide guard-boats to watch this and other channels, so that it was perfectly open to the Americans to send a force against the landing-place, destroy the depots there, and intercept all incoming barges.

Lastly, Lambert's brigade had not yet appeared; and the force on the spot was reduced to fewer than five thousand effective of all ranks. Of these the Fourth and Ninety-Third were strong and excellent; the Twenty-First strong but undisciplined; the Forty-Fourth, only just recruited after heavy losses in the Peninsula, was indifferent; and the Eighty-Fifth and Rifles counted little more than five hundred men between them. The negroes of the West India Regiments, having been sent away without blankets or warm clothing, were so much numbed with cold that they were absolutely useless even for fatigue-duties. For all practical purposes the effective force numbered little, if at all, more than thirty-five hundred of all ranks.

In the depth of his disgust Pakenham used strong language, which was pardonable; but he used it without concealment, so that his opinions filtered down to the privates, which was inexcusable unless he had determined to abandon the enterprise altogether. This, however, it seems that he had not; possibly because he considered persistence in the undertaking, until he had at least dealt the Americans a severe blow, to be the only safe way of extricating his force.

Trustworthy information respecting the enemy's actions was unobtainable, and Jackson's strength was stated by prisoners at any figure from seven to fourteen thousand men. The only method of obtaining intelligence, therefore, was a reconnaissance in force; but, before this could be undertaken, it was necessary to destroy or drive from their stations the two American war-ships on the Mississippi, of which the *Carolina*, by shifting from one bank to the other according to the British changes of position, was a source of constant annoyance though not of serious injury. Accordingly on the 26th, the day after his arrival, Pakenham caused batteries to be erected on the bank with furnaces for heating shot.

The *Carolina* endeavoured to move up the river, but, being foiled by a head wind, was kindled and burned on the 27th. The *Louisiana* was able to shift her position, though by general admission she also might and should have been destroyed; (Harry Smith, *Autobiography*, i.; James, ii.), and she then took up an anchorage under the western bank, abreast of Jackson's entrenchment, so as to sweep the approach to it with a flanking fire.

At dawn of the 28th Pakenham, having reorganised his force into two brigades, advanced with both of them towards the American line. (1st Brigade. Major-General Gibbs: 4th, 21st, 44th, 5th W.I.R.; 2nd Brigade. Major-General Keane: 85th, 93rd, 95th Rifles, 1st W.I.R.).

On arriving within cannon-shot he was greeted with a heavy fire from the battery and from the frigate on the river. Colonel Burgoyne, who accompanied the general, agreed with him that a simple frontal attack was out of the question; and the troops, after suffering a loss of forty or fifty killed or wounded, were withdrawn to a new encampment not more than two miles from the American lines. Detached redoubts were thrown up in advance for the protection of the line pending further operations.

Pakenham now decided that the only possible chance of success was to breach Jackson's breastwork with heavy cannon, and, having done so, to assault. The following days were therefore spent in bringing up ten eighteen-pounder guns and four twenty-four pounder carronades from the ships, a very arduous task, which taxed to the utmost the strength and endurance of the long-suffering seamen.

The American general, of course, was not idle during this interval, continuing to strengthen his foremost entrenchments, to mount additional pieces in them, and to prepare two more lines of defence in rear; while Commodore Patterson of the Louisiana, landing both men and guns on the right bank of the Mississippi, threw shot unceasingly into the British camp. This cannonade, added to constant petty attacks upon the British outposts, to which Jackson wisely never gave five minutes' rest, caused not a few casualties, and contributed materially to wear down the strength and endurance of the invaders.

On the evening of the 31st four eighteen-pounders were placed by the British in battery by the river to keep the *Louisiana* at a distance; and six more, together with four carronades and a battery of field-guns, were mounted as best they could be under the shelter of casks of sugar, within five hundred yards of the enemy's line. The morning of the 1st of January broke with a dense fog, which did not clear until eight o'clock, when the British guns opened fire. The Americans promptly replied, and it was very soon evident that the British pieces were overmatched.

The British projectiles were effectually stopped by the bales of cotton of which the American breastwork was built; whereas the American shot quickly demolished the slender protection thrown up round the British batteries. After a duel of an hour several of the British cannon had been dismounted from their naval carriages, and Pakenham was fain to abandon them and send a party to draw them off under cover of night—a work of great difficulty owing to a heavy fall of rain. The result of the action was a great disappointment to him, as he had issued detailed orders for a general assault, in the expectation that the American artillery would have been speedily silenced.

The absolute failure of this cannonade convinced the British general that the American lines could be forced only by enfilading them from the right bank of the river. On the 2nd and 3rd Commodore Patterson landed more guns from the *Louisiana* on that side, and kept up a more destructive cannonade than ever; and Sir Alexander Cochrane now proposed a very ingenious plan for passing troops over to the right bank, seizing this battery of Patterson's and turning the guns upon Jackson's main line.

The admiral's idea was to widen and deepen the canal, known as Villeré's canal, along which ran the road constructed by the British for purposes of communication, to carry it through the dyke of the Mississippi into the stream, and so to make a direct water-way from the British advanced base to the great river itself. The suggestion was adopted, and the work, being begun at once, was pressed forward with such energy that by the evening of the 6th the naval officers were able to report that everything had been completed to their satisfaction.

★★★★★★

Wylly in his report (*Pakenham Letters*) says that the canal was not begun until the 6th, after the arrival of Lambert s brigade, but this is incredible.

★★★★★★

On that day also arrived Lambert's brigade of the Seventh and Forty-Third, some seventeen hundred strong; and Pakenham matured his schemes for an attack at daylight of the 8th. In the course of the

7th some fifty boats of all sizes were brought into the newly cut canal, and dragged to within a short distance of the Mississippi. The admiral reported that this had been done without the knowledge of the enemy; but the whole movement was perceived by Commodore Patterson from the right bank of the river, and was duly reported by him to Jackson.

The American general, however, appears to have taken no notice of this warning, perhaps because he relied upon an unfinished redoubt, which covered Patterson's battery about half a mile further down stream, to ward off any British attack on that side. This entrenchment was garrisoned by General Morgan with about one thousand militia and two guns; and Jackson contented himself with sending Morgan a few hundred more militia. The event was to prove that this neglect might have cost him very dear.

At nightfall of the 7th, Colonel Thornton with the Eighty-Fifth and a naval brigade of seamen and marines, the latter counting some four hundred men, marched down to the Mississippi to embark on the boats that had been brought down the new water-way by the navy. The time fixed for crossing the river was nine o'clock, and the troops arrived punctually at their appointed station, but found no boats. Hour after hour passed away, and still the boats came not; nor was it until past one in the morning of the 8th that a few of them at last began one by one to make their appearance.

Either the naval officers or the engineers had been deceived in their calculations as to the widening of the canal. The banks, being of soft soil, had given way and blocked the channel about a quarter of a mile from the outlet to the Mississippi, the heaviest of the boats had grounded in this spot, and the whole of the flotilla behind it had been blocked. Pakenham, it is said, had predicted some such misfortune; but whether he had done so or not, the misfortune had come.

★★★★★★

Harry Smith, i. According to this account the canal was on a lower level than the river, and a dam had been constructed to hold the water in the canal when the dyke of the river should be cut through. The dam, as Pakenham had predicted, was too weak to bear the weight of water, and gave way, so that the water ran back and left the boats stranded until the dam could be repaired. Wylly (*Pakenham Letters*) says that the whole of the work on the canal was done under the eyes of the naval officers and approved by them.

★★★★★★

Only with great difficulty and labour were a few boats brought forward, and it was impossible for the rest to follow except after long delay. Thornton was placed in a most difficult position, for the whole success of the operations turned upon him. It had been expected of him to land on the right bank before midnight, storm Morgan's redoubt and Patterson's battery, and train the captured guns upon the flank of the American lines before dawn, so as to be ready to open fire at the signal of a rocket from Pakenham. Now he was already from seven to eight hours late, and only one-third of the appointed number of boats had reached him. Without delay he took his resolution, sent back the whole of his detachment except the Eighty-Fifth and a hundred seamen and marines, and with fewer than four hundred men in all shoved off into the stream. He accepted a great risk, and deserves the highest praise for his enterprise.

On the left bank preparations went on throughout the night of the 7th. Under cover of darkness parties were sent forward to patch up the batteries that had been raised on the 1st, opposite the American right and left; but, as water appeared within a foot of the surface, the men were obliged to pare the soil for a great distance all round in order to obtain earth. Thus the work was but slowly and imperfectly done, and the epaulments were still not shot-proof when six eighteen-pounder guns were, with great exertion, placed within them not long before dawn.

Pakenham's plans were as follows. Over three hundred of the Rifles and as many of the Forty-Fourth were pushed forward very early to occupy these works, and it was ordered that of these six hundred and fifty men four hundred—including three hundred of the Forty-Fourth—were to fire, and the remainder to carry fascines. The officer in command of the Forty-Fourth was further instructed to bring with him sixteen ladders and the fascines aforesaid, and to ascertain in good time where these requisites could be obtained so as to bear them forward with him. Under cover of the firing party and of the carriers of fascines and ladders, the main attack was to be delivered by the Twenty-First and the Fourth under General Gibbs, against the American left, the light companies of the brigade being thrown out to Gibbs's right along the edge of the swamp, so as to protect his right flank.

On the British left the second column, which was entrusted to Keane, was subdivided into two, whose movements were to be guided by the effect of the British artillery upon the American right. On the extreme left the light companies of the Seventh, Forty-Third and Ninety-Third, together with a hundred men of the First West India Regiment, were to advance along the road under command of Colonel Renny; while the bulk of Keane's brigade—which was reduced to the Ninety-Third and the First West India—was to move on the right of Renny and parallel with him, and attack the American right centre, or strike in to the left of Gibbs, according to circumstances.

Both columns were to be covered by such Riflemen—a few score only—as remained over from Gibbs's brigade. The main bodies of the Seventh and Forty-Third under Lambert were held in reserve.

★★★★★★

The accounts of Pakenham's dispositions in Lambert's despatch, and in the narratives of Cooke, Gleig and Surtees, are all different and all wrong. Happily a copy of Pakenham's orders was sent by Keane to Wellington, and is printed together with Keane's journal in *Supp. Desp.* x. That Riflemen did cover Keane's left is shown by Surtees, who is not likely to have misstated the movements of his own regiment, and his story is partly confirmed by Cooke.

★★★★★★

The total number of white troops of all descriptions in line upon both sides of the river was about six thousand rank and file, with six heavy cannon and one battery of field-guns. In addition to these there were about a thousand negro soldiers. The Americans could oppose to this force some six thousand rank and file, with one thirty-two pounder, four twenty-four pounders, one eighteen-pounder and eight smaller guns on the left bank, besides nine heavy guns in Patterson's battery, and two field-pieces in Morgan's redoubt, making in all twenty-five cannon mostly of large calibre.

The whole of the troops fell in at four o'clock and moved up to their appointed stations well before daylight, the foremost skirmishers within one hundred and fifty yards of the American lines, and the Reserve not more than seven hundred yards distant from it. But there had been one grave oversight, for Lieutenant-Colonel Mullens of the Forty-Fourth had led his battalion to its place without bringing with him the ladders and fascines, as had been ordained.

He had, it seems, halted for ten minutes by the redoubt where he had been told to collect them, but, finding no engineer there to give him any information, had marched on under the guidance of a sergeant of artillery to the post assigned to him in the right-hand battery.

175

It was said that this officer had become infected with a spirit like to that which had called down Wellington's wrath upon the Fifth Division at San Sebastian, and had been complaining that his regiment was ordered upon a hopeless venture and was foredoomed to sacrifice.

But this does not necessarily imply deliberate neglect on the part of Mullens; rather it points to a negligence on the part of the staff which was to become only too conspicuous in the course of the day. The mistake was early discovered by General Gibbs, who gave orders for it to be rectified, and reported the circumstance to Pakenham. It was then not yet five o'clock; and Sir Edward at once despatched one of his staff to ascertain the true state of affairs. The staff-officer galloped off on his errand, and shortly before dawn found the Forty-Fourth straggling off to the front from the redoubt where Mullens had halted earlier in the morning, carrying the fascines and ladders in a very irregular and disorderly fashion.

This in the circumstances was not surprising. The battalion, unlike its brother battalion of Wellington's army, was ill-disciplined, and the men had been hurried back at the double over five or six hundred yards of very deep ground, in order to repair an omission which was no fault of their own, with every prospect of being hustled again at the same rate to the front, lest they should be too late for the attack. They were breathless and ill-tempered, the ladders were heavy, and the fascines—made of ripe sugar-cane—very weighty indeed. Moreover, though by right only a small number of them should have been fascine-bearers and three-fourths of them should have been in the firing line, there was every likelihood that the whole of them would be employed in the work which had originally been designed for the Rifles. The staff-officer, however, reported to Pakenham that the battalion would regain its place in good time, and the general rode off, apparently satisfied.

Shortly afterwards he sent for Harry Smith (if that officer's narrative is to be believed), and told him with much agitation of the mishap to Thornton's column, adding that no commander-in-chief had ever had such difficulties to contend with as himself. It was still not quite daylight, and, the ground being covered with thick mist, Smith answered that there was still time to withdraw the troops before they could be seen by the enemy.

"That may be," answered Pakenham, "but I have twice deferred the attack."

Smith continued to argue on the other side, but the general would not listen and gave the order for the signal-rocket to be fired. Even then Smith endeavoured to counsel delay, but Sir Edward was peremptory. The rocket soared into the air, and Gibbs's brigade moved forward in column of companies to the assault, the Twenty-First leading, the Fourth in support, and the Forty-Fourth with the ladders and fascines dispersed all round, breathless and unable to keep up.

The American artillery received the assailants with a terrific crossfire from both sides of the river, and as the storming party, checked at frequent intervals by the drains that ran across the plain, slowly drew nearer, the American musketry wrought havoc in their ranks. So severely were they punished that when within a hundred yards of the enemy's line, they hesitated, and, heedless of the Riflemen, who were skirmishing on their front, began to fire. The Riflemen threw themselves down to escape being shot in the back; and a few of the foremost of the Twenty-First reached the canal that covered the American breastwork, and hunted in vain up and down the bank for a plank or a ladder to enable them to cross it.

One small band of brave men—some say, indeed, two whole companies—under Lieutenant Leavock of the Twenty-First actually traversed the canal, and scrambled up the entrenchment, where Leavock saw nothing before him but two American officers. He summoned them to surrender, but finding himself alone and unsupported was obliged to deliver up his own sword. The main body of the column meanwhile were firing into each other, and rapidly giving way to panic. Gibbs raged among them with oaths and reproaches, but could not stop them.

Pakenham galloped up with his staff to receive Gibbs's despairing report that the troops would not follow him, and directly afterwards Gibbs was struck down by a mortal wound. Pakenham rode among the flying soldiers, vainly striving to rally them. A bullet shattered his knee, and a second bullet killed his horse under him; but he was none the less in the act of mounting a second charger, when he was struck by a third bullet in the spine and in a few minutes expired. Gibbs's brigade then dissolved into a disorderly mass of fugitives, and streamed away to the shelter of the wood on the British right, in rout and demoralisation.

On the British left the three light companies under Renny rushed through a terrific fire upon the advanced redoubt on the right of the American line; and, though two men out of every three fell before they reached the breastwork, the survivors drove out the defenders, captured four guns and ensconced themselves in the exterior ditch (the rear of the redoubt being open) until support should come to them.

The Ninety-Third should have been at hand, but Keane also had been wounded; and the Highlanders, owing to some strange order brought to them during the advance, had been shifted away to the right of Gibbs, where they were halted in close column within musket-shot of the enemy, and under the full blast of their fire. There they stood heroically until some five hundred of them had been killed or wounded, when very pardonably they fell back. Renny's companies, finding themselves isolated and alone, retired from the captured redoubt as best they could, leaving their gallant commander dead behind them; and the entire attack upon the left bank of the river was defeated with disastrous loss, at a cost to the Americans of no more than eight killed and fourteen wounded.

On the right bank Thornton and his little band fared better. As they stepped ashore, they saw the signal-rocket, and pushing on with all haste came after half an hour's march upon an advanced party of Americans. A boat with one carronade in her bow gave these a single round of grape from the river, which sufficed to set them running without further resistance. Continuing his progress, Thornton presently came upon General Morgan's redoubt, and, extending the Eighty-Fifth along the whole length of it as skirmishers, launched his seamen in column against the rampart.

A heavy discharge of grape from two fieldpieces in front and from a battery in flank staggered the blue-jackets for a moment; but, Thornton waving them forward, they rushed on together with the Eighty-Fifth through the smoke of the American cannon. The bare sight of them struck the Kentuckians and the rest of the defenders with terror, and they fled from their formidable stronghold without attempting to fight. Commodore Patterson, finding his battery exposed and defence impossible, spiked his guns and retired; and Thornton saw his task accomplished at no greater sacrifice than that of eighty-three killed and wounded, more than half of whom belonged to the Eighty-Fifth. Being himself among the hurt, Thornton resigned the command to Lieutenant-Colonel Gubbins of the Eighty-Fifth, who pursued the flying enemy for two miles, when the news of the failure of the main attack caused him to halt.

But the tidings of his success had been sufficient to throw Jackson into great perturbation, for the capture of his entrenchments on the

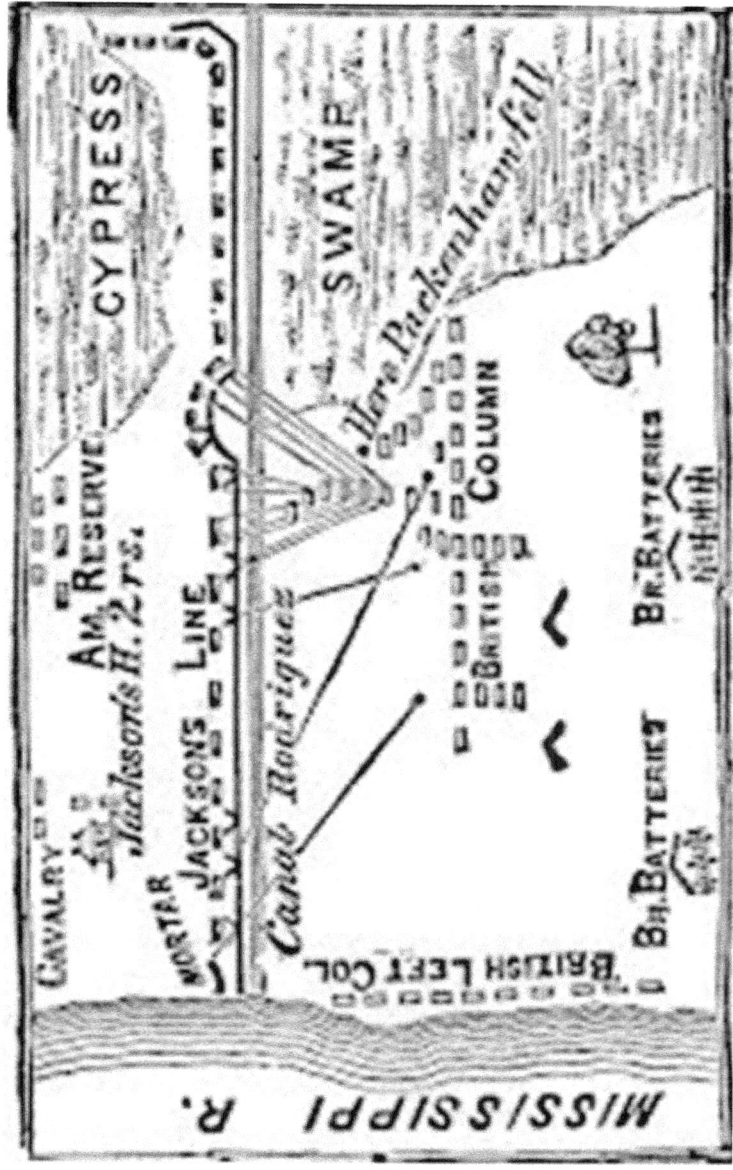

right bank of the Mississippi had given the British (to use his own words) a position from whence they might annoy him without hazard, and even neutralise the repulse of their comrades on the left bank. He was about to set every man that he could spare in motion to regain the lost redoubt, when his anxiety was relieved in a very different fashion.

After the fall of Pakenham, Gibbs, and Keane the chief command devolved upon Lambert, who had landed only two days before, and knew little of Pakenham's plans or expectations except that, according to Sir Edward's calculation, the forcing of the first line of entrenchments would not be the most formidable work of the day. He had still under his hand two superb and well-tried battalions of the Seventh and Forty-Third; but Gibbs's brigade, though it rallied at last far in rear, was irrecoverably demoralised. Lambert brought forward his reserve to cover the retirement of the rest of his troops, and keeping them in that position held a kind of council of war.

The casualties of the army on the left bank alone amounted to close upon two thousand killed, wounded and missing, (295 killed, 1186 wounded, 483 missing = 1964), the last named being for the most part men who had been drowned or had been taken within the American entrenchments. Thus a full third of the force was killed or disabled, and at least another third unfit for further fighting. Three officers only, though the report of Thornton's success was before them, appear to have been in favour of renewing the attack; but only one of these, Colonel John Burgoyne, was entitled to be heard with real respect.

Captain Codrington of the navy, who was in charge of the victualling department, declared that another attack was imperative, otherwise the whole force would be starved.

"Kill plenty more, Admiral," said Harry Smith; "fewer rations will be required."

Ultimately, looking to the danger lest Thornton's detachment should be cut off, and a counter-attack delivered upon the main body, Lambert decided to send in a flag of truce, asking for a suspension of hostilities to bury the dead and collect the wounded, and despatched Colonel Alexander Dickson to the right bank to report upon the situation of Thornton's detachment. The Americans fired upon the flag of truce both with cannon and musketry, but eventually received it; and Jackson eagerly seized the opportunity to grant an armistice until noon of the 9th upon the left bank only, on condition that no reinforcements should be sent to the right bank by either party during the 8th.

Lambert asked for twenty-four hours to consider this proposal, and, receiving Dickson's report that Gubbins could not hold his position in security with fewer than two thousand men, ordered Thornton's detachment to recross the river and rejoin the main body. This was safely effected under cover of a fog; and, after remaining on the ground long enough to destroy his heavy guns, Lambert withdrew his troops through the darkness to their position of the morning, while Jackson eagerly reoccupied his lost entrenchments on the right bank.

Lambert's measures were of course preliminary to a retreat and a re-embarkation; but a retreat was no easy matter. During the advance the soldiers had been brought up the creek in small parties upon the boats of the fleet. These boats were not numerous enough to take more than half of the men at a time; wherefore there was a risk that the moiety embarked might be intercepted, and the moiety left behind might be stranded and overwhelmed. How naval officers could ever have planned a campaign upon such a basis is incomprehensible, yet it is certain that they did so.

It was consequently necessary for Lambert to make a road through a quaking morass in order to march the whole of his men to the shores of Lake Borgne. This arduous work occupied nine entire days, during which Jackson with excellent judgment refrained from any further aggression than an incessant cannonade by day and night, and the despatch of emissaries to tempt the British soldiers to desert. Both methods met with considerable success. The bivouac, already rendered miserable enough by rain all day and frost all night, was made a purgatory by the incessant storm of shot. The men, who were not so much depressed as indignant at their defeat, became sulky and discontented; the Forty-fourth was shunned by all other corps of the army; and, with this quarrelsome and grumbling spirit abroad, many listened to the tempting offers of the Americans and deserted.

At last the road, such as it was, was completed—a mere track covered with faggots of reeds, and bridged by rough branches brought from a distance. At nightfall of the 18th the battalions moved off in dead silence, leaving parties to keep the bivouac-fires alight, and after a short march on the high road entered the track through the swamp. The faggots soon turned to powder under the trampling of many feet, and the weary column struggled on for hours through the starlight, knee-deep in mud at the best of times, and hardly able to get forward at all when a creek was to be passed. More than one man was swallowed up quick in the mire before his comrades' eyes.

However, in the morning the whole arrived, without any molestation from the enemy, at the wretched oasis in the desert of reeds which went by the name of the Fishermen's Huts. Here officers and men threw themselves down upon land rather less unsound than that which they had traversed, and in their drenched and muddy clothes fell asleep from sheer exhaustion.

The boats were at hand to begin the embarkation; but through some miracle of imbecility, which must presumably be ascribed to Captain Codrington, no food had been brought with them except for the crews.

The black corps and Forty-Fourth were embarked, but, as the small craft were from seventy to eighty miles distant from the ships, there was always the chance that foul weather might condemn the force left on shore to starvation. Happily no such trial was in store for the troops. For two days those that remained on the strand of the lake lived on crumbs of biscuit and a minute allowance of rum; but then the boats reappeared, and all anxiety was at an end. Entrenchments were thrown up, although the enemy never showed themselves; and the only additional hardship was the lack of fuel, there being none except reeds, which flared up for a moment and then expired, providing neither warmth nor comfort. Gradually the whole of the soldiers were withdrawn without accident, and by the end of the month all of them were once more aboard the ships, where they found the Fortieth Foot had arrived as a reinforcement.

Bad weather delayed the departure of the fleet until the 5th of February, when Lambert and Cochrane agreed to sail to Mobile, which lies at the head of a bay whose mouth is about fifty miles east of the anchorage at Cat Island. The defences of the place consisted of a small fort, called Fort Bowyer, on the eastern horn of the headland that forms the bay, and of a battery upon the Isle of Dauphiné, which lies across the entrance.

On the 7th the Fourth, Twenty-First and Forty-Fourth were landed, with artillery and engineers, on the peninsula in rear of Fort Bowyer; and the rest of the troops under command of Keane, who had recovered from his wound, were disembarked on the island. On the 8th ground was broken before Fort Bowyer under the direction of Burgoyne and Dickson, and by the morning of the 11th sixteen guns of various calibres were ready to open fire. The *commandant* thereupon surrendered, yielding up a garrison of nearly four hundred of all ranks with twenty-eight guns. The British casualties in this trifling affair just exceeded thirty killed and wounded.

On the 14th a sloop of war arrived with the news that the preliminaries of peace between England and the United States had been signed on the 14th of December 1814, so that all the blood shed before New Orleans had been poured out in vain. The troops remained at the Isle of Dauphiné until the middle of March, when they sailed for England.

So ended this ill-fated expedition, of which it may be said that it provides perhaps the most striking warning upon record to British Ministers against conducting operations ashore upon the sole advice of naval officers. The whole project was based upon the expectation of prize-money only, as truly as were the expeditions to Carthagena in 1740 and to Ferrol in 1800, to mention only two out of many.

A scapegoat had to be found for the mishap, and Lieutenant-colonel Mullens was tried by court-martial and cashiered for disobedience to orders. The man who should have been tried by court-martial and shot was Sir Alexander Cochrane. The callous manner in which he deliberately placed the troops in a most dangerous situation, and then worked his faithful blue-jackets to death to keep them there—all with the principal object of filling his own pockets—cannot be too strongly condemned. He added to these delinquencies the further fault, doubtless also inspired by cupidity, of omitting to inform Lambert immediately of the conclusion of peace, from which cause the return of the troops to Europe, where they were urgently needed, was delayed, (Wellington *Supp. Desp.* x.).

On the other hand the exertions of his officers and men, who had neither rest nor sleep from the moment when Keane's detachment was first landed, who cheerfully endured, through week after week, the endless fatigue of rowing hundreds of miles, drenched every day and frozen every night these cannot be too highly praised.

It remains to examine whether Pakenham made the best of the position, embarrassing and dangerous though it was, in which he found himself upon his arrival. The opinion of his regimental officers was that he might have rushed the American lines at any time, without condescending to silence their cannon, and that he ought to have done so on the 1st of January, if not earlier; for every day's delay enabled the enemy to strengthen his defences and to bring up more guns and troops. On the whole this view was probably sound. Lieutenant Leavock always declared that when he and his few men of the Twenty-First broke into Jackson's lines in the assault of the 8th of January, the whole of the American left was in flight, in fact that assailants and defenders were actually running away from each other in opposite directions at the same moment.

There is nothing incredible in this story, the probable truth of which is confirmed by the panic of Morgan's troops before the attack of Thornton's handful of men on the right bank of the Mississippi. Yet, as the loss would have been heavy, and the consequences of failure possibly annihilation, Pakenham can hardly be blamed if he hesitated, in face of an adverse opinion from such a man as Burgoyne, to take so formidable a risk.

Of the actual attack on the 8th of January, it must be said that the idea of a simultaneous onset upon both banks of the river was masterly in boldness of conception, and should have assured success. The delay in carrying Thornton's force to the right bank was due to the miscalculations of the naval officers and engineers, but, though Thornton's stroke did not fall with the full impetus that Pakenham had designed, it sufficed, as we have seen, to make Jackson almost despair of the situation.

Should Pakenham therefore have delayed the assault upon Jackson's main position until Thornton had carried Patterson's battery? His Military Secretary declared that this would have been fatal. Thornton had crossed the river unobserved thanks only to a mist; and, had the signal been held back, his boats would have returned to bring over a further detachment of his troops. This would probably have led to an engagement of the two flotillas of armed vessels on the river itself; and as the American flotilla was, or at any rate was believed to be, the stronger, it would in all likelihood have destroyed that of the British.

So great was the want of boats in the fleet that such a disaster would not only have left Thornton's little party hopelessly isolated upon the right bank, but would have cut off from the entire force its only means of retreat. The general was in fact hampered in this, as in all other operations, by Cochrane's unpardonable blunder in beginning the enterprise with only half the necessary number of small craft. Had Pakenham been apprised at the outset of the initial failure to launch the boats from the canal into the Mississippi, he would probably have countermanded the whole of his dispositions for the day; but as a matter of fact he knew nothing about it until five o'clock on the morning of the 8th—eight hours after the original difficulty had shown itself—when he judged it to be too late to make any change of plan.

How it came about that he was so long kept in the dark upon this subject has never been explained. The naval officer in charge of the boats should certainly have informed him at once; but this does not acquit both Thornton and Pakenham's own staff-officers of very serious neglect. It was, as we have seen, probably the blunder of a staff-officer that permitted the Forty-Fourth to go forward without their ladders and fascines; it was another staff-officer's blunder which led Pakenham to believe, when he ordered the rocket to be fired, that the Forty-Fourth had had time to fetch its ladders and resume its place at the head of the storming column.

There was no lack of staff-officers in the force, but they seem to have been either inefficient or ill-handled. When all is said and done, however, the main fact remains that the chief reason for the failure of the assault was that the soldiers instead of running forward hung back, began to fire wildly and then ran away. Harry Smith writes in his *Autobiography*:

> It was all very well to victimise old Mullens, the fascines and ladders all could have been supplied by one word, which I will not name.

This one word is obviously courage; and Harry Smith's criticism is amply justified by the success of Renny and Leavock in breaking into the American works. It has therefore been suggested that Pakenham should have chosen the Seventh and Forty-Third, both of them splendid battalions fresh from the Peninsula, to form the main column of attack, instead of two imperfectly disciplined battalions such as the Twenty-First and Forty-Fourth. But this is a question which cannot be discussed without a far more intimate knowledge of the circumstances at the moment than any historian can acquire. It is easy upon paper to set forth a multitude of arguments upon both sides, but it would be utterly unprofitable. The best troops run away, as well as the worst, upon occasion. If it were not so, military history would hardly be worth writing.

As to the correctness of Lambert's decision to abandon further operations and retreat, I think there can be no question. Success in a renewal of the offensive was extremely doubtful; the state of the supplies both for army and navy was extremely dangerous; and above all the object was not worth the risk. The over-worked officers and men of the fleet may well have felt indignant at so humiliating an end to all their labours, but for that they had chiefly to thank their admiral.

The temptations of prize-money as formerly distributed have fortunately been removed from the Fleet, so that we are not likely again to be plunged into disaster by the cupidity of admirals; but it is possible that naval officers have not yet realised their ignorance of the nature of operations ashore. In former days they gave their opinions upon such operations with childish assurance, and by no means the least of the offenders was Nelson himself. There is no nobler service than the Royal Navy; but there are two sentences which should be writ large on the inner walls of the Admiralty and of the Cabinet's meeting-place. Never employ the fleet alone for operations which require the combined forces of army and navy. Never use those combined forces upon the sole advice either of a naval or of a military officer.

For the rest, the treaty of peace brought no advantage either to England or to the United States. The former gained no rectification of the frontier; the latter no satisfaction for captures, nor abandonment of the English doctrine concerning the impressment of sailors, which was the pretext alleged for American aggression. Upon a general balance of the results of the actual fighting by sea and by land, there was little to be claimed in favour of either party; but, in the matter of injury inflicted, the Americans, owing to the losses caused by the British naval blockade, suffered incomparably more than the British. They were in fact utterly exhausted.

Each country, however, learned respect for the other; and, in spite of much abusive language wasted on both sides by scribblers of all descriptions, the actual combatants in the field treated each other with humanity and even with friendliness. Commodore Barney, when he was taken prisoner, was received, to use his own words, "like a brother" by the British naval officers; and Jackson proved himself to be not only brave and able as a commander, but courteous in negotiation, modest in reporting his own achievements, and kind and considerate to the British wounded who fell into his hands.

His countrymen in New Orleans emulated his example in the matter of the wounded with a generosity that did them infinite honour; and thus the repulse by the Mississippi, though the most crushing blow that was sustained by the British Army in the course of the war, left behind it less bitterness than any other. Upon the whole the war, through the military failures on both sides, the early successes of the American frigates, and the final exhausting pressure of the British fleet upon American sea-borne trade, revealed to both nations their

strength and their weakness, and did more than is suspected to pre-
serve peace inviolate between them for a hundred years.

LEONAUR

ALSO FROM LEONAUR
AVAILABLE IN SOFTCOVER OR HARDCOVER WITH DUST JACKET

AN APACHE CAMPAIGN IN THE SIERRA MADRE *by John G. Bourke*—An Account of the Expedition in Pursuit of the Chiricahua Apaches in Arizona, 1883.

BILLY DIXON & ADOBE WALLS *by Billy Dixon and Edward Campbell Little*—Scout, Plainsman & Buffalo Hunter, *Life and Adventures of "Billy" Dixon* by Billy Dixon and *The Battle of Adobe Walls* by Edward Campbell Little (*Pearson's Magazine*).

WITH THE CALIFORNIA COLUMN *by George H. Petis*—Against Confederates and Hostile Indians During the American Civil War on the South Western Frontier, *The California Column, Frontier Service During the Rebellion* and *Kit Carson's Fight With the Comanche and Kiowa Indians*.

THRILLING DAYS IN ARMY LIFE *by George Alexander Forsyth*—Experiences of the Beecher's Island Battle 1868, the Apache Campaign of 1882, and the American Civil War.

THE NEZ PERCÉ CAMPAIGN, 1877 *by G. O. Shields & Edmond Stephen Meany*—Two Accounts of Chief Joseph and the Defeat of the Nez Percé, *The Battle of Big Hole* by G. O. Shields and *Chief Joseph, the Nez Percé* by Edmond Stephen Meany.

CAPTAIN JEFF OF THE TEXAS RANGERS *by W. J. Maltby*—Fighting Comanche & Kiowa Indians on the South Western Frontier 1863-1874.

SHERIDAN'S TROOPERS ON THE BORDERS *by De Benneville Randolph Keim*—The Winter Campaign of the U. S. Army Against the Indian Tribes of the Southern Plains, 1868-9.

GERONIMO *by Geronimo*—The Life of the Famous Apache Warrior in His Own Words.

WILD LIFE IN THE FAR WEST *by James Hobbs*—The Adventures of a Hunter, Trapper, Guide, Prospector and Soldier.

THE OLD SANTA FE TRAIL *by Henry Inman*—The Story of a Great Highway.

LIFE IN THE FAR WEST *by George F. Ruxton*—The Experiences of a British Officer in America and Mexico During the 1840's.

ADVENTURES IN MEXICO AND THE ROCKY MOUNTAINS *by George F. Ruxton*—Experiences of Mexico and the South West During the 1840's.

AVAILABLE ONLINE AT **www.leonaur.com**
AND FROM ALL GOOD BOOK STORES
07/09

LEONAUR

ALSO FROM LEONAUR

AVAILABLE IN SOFTCOVER OR HARDCOVER WITH DUST JACKET

THE ART OF WAR *by Antoine Henri Jomini*—Strategy & Tactics From the Age of Horse & Musket.

THE ART OF WAR *by Sun Tzu and Pierre G. T. Beauregard*—*The Art of War* by Sun Tzu and *Principles and Maxims of the Art of War* by Pierre G.T. Beauregard.

THE MILITARY RELIGIOUS ORDERS OF THE MIDDLE AGES *by F. C. Woodhouse*—The Knights Templar, Hospitaller and Others.

THE BENGAL NATIVE ARMY *by F. G. Cardew*—An Invaluable Reference Resource.

ARTILLERY THROUGH THE AGES—*by Albert Manucy*—A History of the DEvelopment and Use of Cannons, Mortars, Rockets & Projectiles from Earliest Times to the Nineteenth Century.

THE SWORD OF THE CROWN *by Eric W. Sheppard*—A History of the British Army to 1914.

THE 7TH (QUEEN'S OWN) HUSSARS: Volume 3—1818-1914 *by C. R. B. Barrett*—On Campaign During the Canadian Rebellion, the Indian Mutiny, the Sudan, Matabeleland, Mashonaland and the Boer War Volume 3: 1818-1914.

THE CAMPAIGN OF WATERLOO *by Antoine Henri Jomini*—A Political & Military History from the French perspective.

RIFLE & DRILL *by S. Bertram Browne*—The Enfield Rifle Musket, 1853 and the Drill of the British Soldier of the Mid-Victorian Period *A Companion to the New Rifle Musket* and *A Practical Guide to Squad and Setting-up Dtill.*

NAPOLEON'S MEN AND METHODS *by Alexander L. Kielland*—The Rise and Fall of the Emperor and His Men Who Fought by His Side.

THE WOMAN IN BATTLE *by Loreta Janeta Velazquez*—Soldier, Spy and Secret Service Agent for the Confederancy During the American Civil War.

THE BATTLE OF ORISKANY 1777 *by Ellis H. Roberts*—The Conflict for the Mowhawk Valley During the American War of Independenc.

PERSONAL RECOLLECTIONS OF JOAN OF ARC *by Mark Twain.*

CAESAR'S ARMY *by Harry Pratt Judson*—The Evolution, Composition, Tactics, Equipment & Battles of the Roman Army.

FREDERICK THE GREAT & THE SEVEN YEARS' WAR *by F. W. Longman.*

AVAILABLE ONLINE AT **www.leonaur.com**
AND FROM ALL GOOD BOOK STORES

07/09

![LEONAUR]

ALSO FROM LEONAUR
AVAILABLE IN SOFTCOVER OR HARDCOVER WITH DUST JACKET

THE WOMAN IN BATTLE *by Loreta Janeta Velazquez*—Soldier, Spy and Secret Service Agent for the Confederacy During the American Civil War.

BOOTS AND SADDLES *by Elizabeth B. Custer*—The experiences of General Custer's Wife on the Western Plains.

FANNIE BEERS' CIVIL WAR *by Fannie A. Beers*—A Confederate Lady's Experiences of Nursing During the Campaigns & Battles of the American Civil War.

LADY SALE'S AFGHANISTAN *by Florentia Sale*—An Indomitable Victorian Lady's Account of the Retreat from Kabul During the First Afghan War.

THE TWO WARS OF MRS DUBERLY *by Frances Isabella Duberly*—An Intrepid Victorian Lady's Experience of the Crimea and Indian Mutiny.

THE REBELLIOUS DUCHESS *by Paul F. S. Dermoncourt*—The Adventures of the Duchess of Berri and Her Attempt to Overthrow French Monarchy.

LADIES OF WATERLOO *by Charlotte A. Eaton, Magdalene de Lancey & Juana Smith*—The Experiences of Three Women During the Campaign of 1815: Waterloo Days by Charlotte A. Eaton, A Week at Waterloo by Magdalene de Lancey & Juana's Story by Juana Smith.

NURSE AND SPY IN THE UNION ARMY *by Sarah Emma Evelyn Edmonds*—During the American Civil War

WIFE NO. 19 *by Ann Eliza Young*—The Life & Ordeals of a Mormon Woman During the 19th Century

DIARY OF A NURSE IN SOUTH AFRICA *by Alice Bron*—With the Dutch-Belgian Red Cross During the Boer War

MARIE ANTOINETTE AND THE DOWNFALL OF ROYALTY *by Imbert de Saint-Amand*—The Queen of France and the French Revolution

THE MEMSAHIB & THE MUTINY *by R. M. Coopland*—An English lady's ordeals in Gwalior and Agra during the Indian Mutiny 1857

MY CAPTIVITY AMONG THE SIOUX INDIANS *by Fanny Kelly*—The ordeal of a pioneer woman crossing the Western Plains in 1864

WITH MAXIMILIAN IN MEXICO *by Sara Yorke Stevenson*—A Lady's experience of the French Adventure

AVAILABLE ONLINE AT **www.leonaur.com**
AND FROM ALL GOOD BOOK STORES
07/09

www.ingramcontent.com/pod-product-compliance
Lightning Source LLC
Chambersburg PA
CBHW021059090426
42738CB00006B/412

* 9 7 8 1 7 8 2 8 2 4 9 2 3 *